NORTH AMERICAN **ICELANDIC**:
the life of a language

NORTH AMERICAN **ICELANDIC:**
the life of a language

Birna Arnbjörnsdóttir

University of Manitoba Press

© Birna Arnbjörnsdottír 2006
University of Manitoba Press
Winnipeg Manitoba R3T 2N2 Canada
www.umanitoba.ca/uofmpress

All rights reserved. No part of this publication may be reproduced or transmitted in any form or by any means, or stored in a database and retrieval system, without the prior written permission of University of Manitoba Press, or, in the case of photocopying or other reprographic copying, a licence from ACCESS COPYRIGHT (Canadian Copyright Licensing Agency), 6 Adelaide Street East, Suite 900, Toronto, Ontario M5C 1H6, www.accesscopyright.ca.

Cover and text design: Relish Design Studio

Library and Archives Canada Cataloguing in Publication

Arnbjörnsdóttir, Birna, 1952-
    North American Icelandic : the life of a language / Birna Arnbjornsdottir.

Includes bibliographical references and index.
ISBN 0-88755-694-9 (pbk.)

    1. Icelandic language – North America – History. I. Title.

PD2409.A75 2006   439.6097   C2006-905266-2

University of Manitoba Press gratefully acknowledges the financial support for its publication program provided by the Government of Canada through the Book Publishing Industry Development Program (BPIDP), the Canada Council for the Arts, the Manitoba Arts Council, and the Manitoba Department of Culture, Heritage, and Tourism.

Publication of this book has been made possible through a grant from the Icelandic Language and Literature Fund, Icelandic Department at the University of Manitoba.

For my children

TABLE OF **CONTENTS**

INTRODUCTION 3

1 HISTORICAL BACKGROUND 13

2 THE LIFE CYCLE OF NORTH AMERICAN ICELANDIC 35

3 THE NORTH AMERICAN ICELANDIC LEXICON 53

4 COLLECTING THE DATA 73

5 THE GRAMMAR OF NORTH AMERICAN ICELANDIC 87

6 PERCEIVED VOWEL MERGERS:
   IDENTIFICATION OF THE VARIABLES 113

7 THE SPREAD OF FLÁMÆLI IN NORTH AMERICAN ICELANDIC 133

BIBLIOGRAPHY 153

NORTH AMERICAN **ICELANDIC:**
the life of a language

INTRODUCTION

In the last decade, interest in the history of the Icelandic immigrants in North America has incr eased considerably. Over the years, scholarly works and fictional accounts depicting the lives of the immigrants have been written and published in Canada, where most of them settled. More recently, Icelanders have brought the immigrant experiences to the screen, in television and films, and immigrants have been the topics of books and articles. To date, none of this work has focussed specifically on the language developed by the immigrants, which clearly reflects their existence in the new world and separates itself in significant ways from the language varieties spoken in Iceland. This book is an effort to fill that gap.

Below, linguistic data is p resented that describes North American Icelandic, which is sp oken mainly in I celandic settlements in M anitoba, Canada, and in N orth Dakota, in t he United States. The book offers a description of the linguistic and social features that separate this variety, the only one spoken outside Iceland, from the varieties spoken in Iceland. The influence of the two main causes of change in N orth American (NA) Icelandic—intensive contact with English and the status of NA Icelandic as a dying language variety—is considered specifically for the effects on its lexicon, morphology, phonology, and syntax.

The book is a revised and updated version of my doctoral thesis submitted to the University of Texas at Austin, Texas, in 1990. The thesis examined the influence of fifteen social and linguistic factors on the development of a specific phonological feature of North American Icelandic called Flámæli.

The book differs from the original dissertation in purpose, scope, and intended audience. Although the core intent remains unchanged—to provide information about North American Icelandic—a dissertation's purpose is to demonstrate the candidate's ability to conduct research and to place the results within the larger context of relevant scholarship. This book's purpose is to inform the reader about the development and characteristics of North American Icelandic. Therefore, some of the technical detail pertaining to the theoretical context and methodology of data collection has been simplified in this version in favour of a shorter general description. An interested reader can access the details in the dissertation itself. Also, no background in linguistics is required of the readers of this book, so efforts have been made to eliminate jargon and a definition of terminology is provided where deemed necessary.

The scope of the book is somewhat broader than the dissertation's. The original study conducted in 1986 was prompted by the need to document North American Icelandic before it died out, as well as to consolidate the limited and scattered information available about the nature and development of this variety of Icelandic.

Secondly, and this was the main focus of the original doctoral thesis, the book examines in some detail the social and linguistic constraints that affected the development of one specific feature of NA Icelandic phonology undergoing change, namely Flámæli. Flámæli refers to the apparent mergers of two sets of front vowels; on the one hand (I) and (E), and on the other hand their rounded counterparts (Y) and (ö). Variable rule analysis with the aid of the Goldvarb computer program was employed to determine precisely which linguistic and social constraints condition the appearance or non-appearance of Flámæli in an individual's speech. The basic questions were: how widespread was Flámæli; how did it spread, socially and linguistically;

and what, if anything, could the results tell us about the nature of Flámæli? The rationale for choosing Flámæli for further examination will be discussed below.

It is generally acknowledged that Icelandic is a conservative language. This is thought to be due to its geographical isolation, the close-knit network of its speakers, their identification with literature and traditions expressed in older forms of the language, and strong linguistic preservation forces. One of the most successful efforts in language "preservation" was a public and official movement around the middle of the previous century to eradicate the apparent mergers of two sets of four front vowels—that is, the feature popularly known as Flámæli or "skewed speech." The "mergers" created homonyms that were thought to hamper communication, the 'confusion' being carried over into the orthography (Björn Guðfinnsson 1981). Flámæli became the only dialect feature in Icelandic, possibly in the world, to be stigmatized and, through official efforts, to be eradicated. The result was that Flámæli, previously a pronounced feature of three regional dialects in Iceland, is no longer considered a feature of modern Icelandic in its original form (Þórunn Blöndal 1985; Höskuldur Þráinsson and Kristján Árnason 1984; and others).

Flámæli was probably widespread in at least one of the areas of Iceland that saw most emigration to North America in the latter part of the nineteenth century. Icelandic continued to be spoken in the Icelandic immigrant communities in rural Saskatchewan and Manitoba in Canada and in North Dakota in the United States. About 15,000 people are thought to have emigrated, most settling initially in "New Iceland," a tract of land on the shores of Lake Winnipeg that was reserved for Icelanders alone. New Iceland was self-governing for almost a decade with its own government fashioned after Icelandic traditions and with laws written in Icelandic. The Icelandic immigrants kept up the tradition of home schooling but established English schools immediately upon arrival. Bilingualism was the norm and Icelandic has been preserved in these communities beyond the three-generation paradigm, the characteristic survival time of immigrant languages in North America. Icelandic in North America has diverged enough from Icelandic to be considered a dialect in its own right (Haraldur Bessason 1984a).

In NA Icelandic, Flámæli has developed and spread unchecked by the preservation forces that reversed its spread in Icelandic in Iceland. Thus, studying NA Icelandic affords us an opportunity to view this possible vowel merger in progress and use those findings to explain the linguistic and social constraints that may have influenced the nature and spread of Flámæli in Iceland. Also, such findings add to our knowledge of apparent vowel mergers in general.

The cause, nature, and reasons for the fast spread of Flámæli in Icelandic in Iceland have been a matter of dispute. Early studies from the 1940s (Björn Guðfinnsson 1946, 1964) were hampered by the fact that they took place before the availability of the tape recorder. More recent studies have either been conducted *post-facto*, or based on Björn Guðfinnsson's data. Most scholars have suggested that Flámæli is part of a continuous shift within the Icelandic vowel system towards a simpler and more equidistant system (Magnús Pétursson 1978). More recent studies have suggested that there may be other forces involved in the "mergers," such as diphthongization. Scholars are also beginning to investigate the social context of Flámæli (Þórunn Blöndal 1985; Höskuldur Þráinsson and Kristján Árnason 1984). These studies indicate that there may be a new version of Flámæli emerging among young speakers in Reykjavík.

The final goal of the book is to offer a possible explanation of the life cycle of North American Icelandic from its inception to its eventual demise. The forces that led to its development and maintenance are discussed and those that will lead to its eventual attrition as a separate dialect of Icelandic are described. It is suggested that after 1974, when communication between Iceland and the immigrants' communities in North America increased, and as the native speakers of the dialect die out, the two dialects have actually converged and thus some of the features characteristic of North American Icelandic at the time of the study in 1986 may no longer exist. This makes the publication and thus the preservation of the data even more relevant today.

WHY ARE FLÁMÆLI AND NORTH AMERICAN ICELANDIC OF INTEREST TO SCHOLARS?

This is the most comprehensive general description of NA Icelandic available and most likely the last one, as the language is in the last stages of attrition.

The description is comprehensive in that it incorporates the few previous efforts at describing the language, most notably by Haraldur Bessason (1967 and 1984a, 1984b, 1984c), and considers data from two unpublished interviews by Gísli Sigurðsson (1982) and Hallfreður Örn Eiríksson (1974). This effort thus adds to the existing literature on immigrant languages in the United States and Canada and to the discussion on how languages diverge and die out altogether.

Vowel mergers and falsely reported vowel mergers have been a research interest of many scholars throughout the history of linguistics, among them Martinet (1952), Labov, Yeager, and Steiner (1972), Nunberg (1980), Trudgill (1983), Harris (1985), and others. The nature of vowel mergers, the reasons why seemingly merged vowels split again, and how mergers interact with other linguistic phenomena such as diphthongization are not well understood. This study is an effort to give input to that discussion.

Investigating apparent vowel mergers or Flámæli in NA Icelandic affords us a unique opportunity to follow the linguistic development of this specific phonological feature, free of official and public stigma, under conditions that accelerated its spread. Flámæli was brought to the New World in the speech of the immigrants who left Iceland in the late nineteenth century, half a century prior to the "purification" efforts that targetted Flámæli as an undesirable speech marker. Flámæli in Icelandic in Iceland and in NA Icelandic is seen as the same process, although the possible influences from English in NA Icelandic are not ignored.

Several research questions are proposed as to the nature of variation within NA Icelandic based on its socio-historical context. Given the scarcity of literature on NA Icelandic, many of these are based on studies conducted on Flámæli in Iceland as well as on a pilot study undertaken as a precursor to the research presented here. The hypotheses that have been formulated based on the questions posed are twofold: hypotheses about the linguistic context of Flámæli; and hypotheses about the social context of Flámæli. Of specific interest are questions concerning the influences of vowel length and the nature of the linguistic environment on the appearance of Flámæli. Also, this study asked whether the frequency and spread of Flámæli in speech varied according to geographical location, age, and gender.

The final goal is to contribute to the discussion about the interplay between language and society in Iceland. The study of the social context of Icelandic is in its infancy. Linguistic attitudes in Iceland have changed and research orientation has broadened to include interest in the social context of language use. In the last four to five decades, Icelandic has changed from an isolated, largely rural speech community to a modern urban society in a community of other nations. The previously tightly knit familial networks have given way to a more complex, modern societal structure. Modern Icelanders seem to look to the future more than to the past. Communications with the rest of the world have accelerated at all levels of society. Icelandic, like other small languages, is under pressure from English, which threatens to take over the periphery of the language's functional range; namely, in highly specific areas of academia, international business, and technology. Thus, linguistic and social pressures from the outside increase and linguistic conservatism has given way to more modern attitudes about language evolution and language change.

North American Icelandic has developed within a vastly different context in its 125-year history as an immigrant language from the context of the development of Icelandic in Iceland. Yet it shares the close encounter with English, albeit in a more intensely integrative way. The different contexts—in the case of NA Icelandic, the vastly accelerated language contact—may give us insights into the past and possibly the future evolution of Icelandic as the context of its usage changes. Studying North American Icelandic with its "looser" knit ties to Icelandic culture and identity thus gives us interesting insights into the possible future evolution of Icelandic in Iceland.

ORGANIZATION OF THE BOOK

The book may be divided into two sections. The first section (chapters 1 to 3) contains a general description of the linguistic and social context of North American Icelandic and is based on data from various sources. The second half (chapters 4 to 7) is more linguistically oriented and devoted mainly to the examination of Flámæli.

Chapter 1 contains the linguistic and socio-historical precursors to the development of North American Icelandic. The social, cultural, and economic conditions in Iceland and the timing of the immigrations are described as laying the foundation for the development of North American Icelandic and culture.

Chapter 2 describes the life cycle of North American Icelandic, from the social and linguistic forces that led to its inception to the forces that will lead to its demise. The chapter also illustrates the unique position the Icelandic immigrants in Canada and North America held vis-à-vis other immigrant groups. The timing of the immigration was advantageous. The tradition of home education, literacy, and personality traits that are by-products of ethnic pride are seen as having encouraged bilingualism and biculturalism longer than among most other immigrant groups in North America. So did the fact that the host culture and the home culture were not seen as conflicting by the Icelandic immigrants. The chapter ends with a discussion of how the narrowing functional range, rather than the deterioration of the grammar and vocabulary of NA Icelandic, will lead to its attrition.

Chapter 3 consolidates data and information about the lexicon of NA Icelandic. Haraldur Bessason discussed the lexicon of NA Icelandic in his 1967 article, so vocabulary was not a focus of my original study. However, I did include in this book a list of lexical items that appear in the various sources with some consistency and frequency. My discussion is heavily indebted to Haraldur Bessason's 1967 article.

Chapter 4 begins with a discussion of the research methodology and analytical tools used in the study of Flámæli, and provides a non-technical description of methods of accessing sociolinguistic data as proposed originally by Labov (1972a, 1972b) and others. The two communities that served as research sites for this study are identified and described; procedures for selecting informants are also included. Characteristics of the informants are presented as well as some issues pertaining to accessing appropriate speech samples.

Chapter 5 contains a preliminary description of characteristic features of phonology, morphology, and syntax of North American Icelandic. Most of the features are presented unanalyzed, with general suggestions for further research. This consolidation effort has generated more questions than it has answered and, I hope, will be a fertile source of further investigation of this immigrant language.

Chapter 6 defines the research problem, introduces the variables, and presents an overview of the conclusions of studies of Flámæli in Iceland. These studies, as well as a pilot study to the research reported here, guided the choice of social and linguistic factor groups that are identified as influencing the occurrence or non-occurrence of Flámæli in North American Icelandic. Each factor and factor group and their effect is discussed individually.

In Chapter 7, I place the research problem within a larger theoretical framework and issues concerning vowel mergers and apparent mergers (Labov, Yeager, and Steiner 1972). A short overview of the actual quantification procedures, results, and interpretations is provided. The findings of this study are compared to findings of other similar studies of Flámæli in Iceland. A hypothesis about the nature of Flámæli is put forth where Flámæli is presented as a two-part process, the interaction of vowel lowering and diphthongization. Finally, the tabulations of the influences of social factors on Flámæli are discussed. The last section of the chapter holds the general conclusions drawn from the NA Icelandic data along with suggestions for further study. Possible explanations for the nature and causes of Flámæli are synthesized based on the research findings. Some limitations of this type of study are discussed and important implications for further research of the social constraints that affect the future of Icelandic in North America and the development of Icelandic in Iceland are presented.

NOMENCLATURE

1. The terms *language*, *dialect*, and *variety* are used interchangeably in this book. No clear definitions of these terms exist, although the term *language* usually refers to a language that separates itself in significant ways from other languages to the point that they are not mutually intelligible. This, of course, is problematic as we talk about Chinese dialects, most of which are not mutually intelligible, and the Scandinavian languages, which are. Linguists prefer to use the term *variety*, as it does not denote any type of hierarchical relationship among different varieties of a language in a way that the term *dialect* implies. In this view, for example, Standard American English is just another variety within the group of varieties that make up the English language. The same is true for Scottish English and any

other variety of English. The term *variety* does not assume that one variety is more correct or better or a deviation from any other variety.

2. The variety of Icelandic described here is called *North American Icelandic*. It has often been referred to as *Western Icelandic*. In English, the name *Western Icelandic* is misleading, as it seems to denote a variety of Icelandic that is spoken in the western part of Iceland.

3. In accordance with Icelandic custom, in-text citations contain full names of Icelandic authors. In the bibliography, all authors are alphabetized according to their last names.

CHAPTER 1 **HISTORICAL BACKGROUND**

In presenting the history of the Icelanders in North America as it pertains to the survival of their language, it is necessary to recount some of the shared cultural and linguistic traditions of Icelanders that laid the foundations for their cultural activities in the New World. This is followed by a short description of variation (or lack thereof) in Icelandic. Then the causes and events that led to emigration and resettlement of Icelanders in North America are discussed, as well as their settlement history, for these are intricately woven into the history of their language. In the next chapter these events will be directly related to the development of North American Icelandic from inception to attrition.

A STATISTICAL OVERVIEW OF SPEAKERS OF NORTH AMERICAN ICELANDIC

The history of the Icelandic settlement in North America is somewhat unique in that the original immigrants came to the New World with the intention of forming a "New Iceland" where all Icelanders could settle in a more hospitable environment than their homeland had become. Approximately 15,000

Icelanders are thought to have settled in the United States and Canada from 1873 to 1914, when immigration was reduced to a trickle (Júníus Kristjánsson 1983).

In 1986, when the data for this study were gathered, the variety of Icelandic spoken in the Icelandic settlements of North America was a dying immigrant language with few speakers under fifty years old. It is still spoken mainly in the Interlake region to the east between Lake Winnipeg and Lake Manitoba in Manitoba, around Wynyard in northern Saskatchewan in Canada, and in parts of Pembina County in northern North Dakota in the United States. The number of speakers is not known, but according to the Canadian census from 1986, when this study was conducted, out of a 20% data sample, 14,470 persons in Canada as a whole were of Icelandic ethnic origin and, of those, 6980 lived in Manitoba. Of those, 305 claimed that Icelandic was their first language and 800 said they had grown up with English and Icelandic as home languages. In 1986 there is a dramatic decline in numbers from previous censuses. This is likely due to lack of interest in one's ethnic origins, typically found in the second and third generation of immigrants. It is, however, safe to assume that the numbers of those who still spoke Icelandic declined. Most of the speakers and the informants for this study were over fifty in 1986, and were second-, third-, and fourth-generation Icelandic Canadians or Icelandic Americans.

The table below shows the growth of the Icelandic population in Manitoba from 1881 to 2001 (based in part on Salus 1971, p. 237).

TABLE 1
Growth of the Icelandic Population in Manitoba from 1881–2001

Year	Icelandic Background	Total Population of Manitoba
1881	773	65,954
1921	11,043	610,118
1931	9544	700,139
1951	13,649	776,541
1961	14,547	921,686
1986	6980	1,071,232
1996	25,735	1,100,295
2001	26,480	1,103,695

This table indicates the number of people in Manitoba and thus only partially represents the numbers of persons of Icelandic descent in North America. The low number of Icelanders in Manitoba in 1881 is due to the fact that for two to three years before, there had been an exodus of Icelanders from New Iceland, Manitoba, to North Dakota and to Saskatchewan.

According to the census of 1931, there were 19,382 persons who claimed Icelandic ancestry in all of Canada. Of those, 82% listed Icelandic as their primary language and 73% were born in North America. At that time 7413 people of Icelandic extraction were in the US. By 1941, 73% of those claiming Icelandic ancestry in Canada seem to have claimed Icelandic as their first language. However, included in that percentage is quite a number of Irish speakers from Quebec who put down *Irlandais*, which was interpreted as *Islandais* by census officials. It is not known if the opposite also occurred; i.e., *Islandais* was interpreted as *Irlandais* (Haraldur Bessason 1967). By 1961 the numbers of people of Icelandic descent had risen to 30,623 in Canada and 8669 in the US. It is difficult to determine the accuracy of these numbers, and impossible to determine how many of these people still spoke Icelandic at that time. The 1996 census for the whole of Canada did not have a category for Icelandic ethnic origin, but the numbers in Manitoba alone had risen to 25,735 (up from 6980 in 1986) for those who had Icelandic ancestry on one side and 4785 who claimed to be of Icelandic background on both sides. This rise in numbers of Icelandic ancestry is unlikely to be due to a spurt of fertility in the population, but rather an indication of the increased interest that third- and fourth-generation immigrants have in their origins. It is a sign that the assimilation process is near completion or complete. In the census from 2001, there were not enough, if any, speakers of Icelandic to warrant a separate category and the numbers are therefore unavailable. It is an indication of how few speakers are left, though, that some of the specific language categories had as few as seventy speakers (<www.statcan.ca>).

Many scholars have commented on the remarkable survival of Icelandic in North America, given the relatively few numbers of original settlers of Icelandic extraction and the fact that immigration ceased in 1914 (Haraldur Bessason 1984a; Haugen 1956). "Remarkable survival" may be somewhat strong terms to describe the survival of Icelandic. Icelandic has survived beyond the traditional three-generation paradigm (Ferguson 1959) in that many third- and fourth-generation Icelandic Canadians and Icelandic Americans still spoke the language in 1986. The survival of the language beyond the third generation is interesting as there has been no continuation of immigration and thus not a constant influx of new immigrants to sustain the language in the new world. However, Icelandic is spoken mainly by the oldest members of the community in rural areas where Icelanders used to be the dominant language group and in later years by people who have made an effort to learn modern Icelandic through more formal ways. The Icelandic of those who learned the language "at their mother's knee" shows signs of influence from English in the lexicon, phonology, morphology, and syntax as well as signs of attrition, although in 1986 these were less than expected. But there is every reason to believe, as the demographics indicate, that North American Icelandic will follow many other immigrant languages from that period in North American immigrant history into oblivion.

During the first decade in the new world the Icelandic settlers had their own government, answering only to the federal government in Ottawa. They had their own laws, schools, and newspapers. In addition, the Icelandic immigrants brought with them a cultural tradition and ethnicity defined in terms of the language and literature, a general literacy, and an emphasis on home education (Vilhjálmur Stefánsson 1903; Haraldur Bessason 1967, 1984a, 1984b, 1984c). Consequently, most of second- and third-generation Icelanders in Canada not only spoke Icelandic as children, but many could also read and write Icelandic before they had formal education. There was a great deal of literary activity in the Icelandic community and some of the best-loved poets writing in the Icelandic language around the turn of the century were Icelandic Canadians. Today, however, North American Icelandic is mainly a "home language" among the oldest generation, while English is the medium for transactions outside the family and with younger persons.

CULTURAL AND LINGUISTIC BACKGROUND

Central to the understanding of the Icelandic national character is the view that Icelanders see their cultural heritage in terms of their language. Through their language, their own history and culture from the period of settlement in the ninth century were documented, as well as that of Scandinavia. Much of this oral history was written down in the twelfth and thirteenth centuries in a body of literature that came to be known as the Icelandic Sagas. During the same period, *The First Grammatical Treatise* was written. The *Treatise* is the first detailed description of the structure of Icelandic written in Old Icelandic (Hreinn Benediktsson 1972). This literature has provided the foundation of Icelandic culture and heritage.

To Icelanders the Sagas not only symbolized national pride and unity, "they also exemplified Icelandic in its purest form" (Gísli Pálsson 1989, p. 3). Preserving the Icelandic language equalled preserving the Icelandic culture. Gísli Pálsson further contends: "Icelanders tend to regard their language not as an extension of their person or a culturally-fashioned tool, but rather as an artifact independent of themselves analogous to their equally celebrated landscape—in other words, an external condition within which they operate" (1989, p. 3). The view that the Icelandic language somehow had an existence separate from its speakers was shared by prominent scholars, as well as the general public, and permeated the discussion on language preservation in Iceland from the middle age up until the last decades of the last century. Conserving the cultural artefact that was and is the Icelandic language equalled conserving a separate Icelandic cultural identity. This linguistic heritage provided a reference point against which Icelanders' identity has been measured through the centuries. This sense of identity and connection with the language and literature seems to have been in stark contrast to their poor external condition. The duality in terms of how the Icelanders saw themselves vis-à-vis how they were viewed by the outside world seems also to have served them well in the New World.

The earliest accounts of expressions of linguistic purism in Iceland date back to 1609, when Arngrímur Jónsson the Learned called for the necessity to preserve the "purity" of Icelandic (in Gísli Pálsson 1989, p. 2). By the eighteenth century this view had found structure and support in an influential nationalistic organization called The Icelandic Society for the Learned Arts. The society had popular support and, according to Halldór Halldórsson (1979), two main agendas, which have characterized the purism movement in Iceland up until the latter part of the twentieth century. The first agenda was "the respect for the language and its purity" (p. 77), and the second was that the language in its purest form should be spoken by all Icelanders irrespective of education or social status, and scholarly articles should be written in language that "was easy to understand for the common people" (Halldór Halldórsson 1979, p. 79). The latter point indicates at least a perceived general literacy and access to scholarly works by the general public in Iceland.

Halldór Halldórsson further contends that "an increased nationalism and the struggle for independence from Denmark, along with the Romantic Movement in the nineteenth century, strengthened the purism forces" (Halldór Halldórsson 1979, p. 80). With the growing desire for independence came efforts to uproot Danish influences from Icelandic. The Romantic era brought further efforts to imitate and re-establish the Old Icelandic style of the Sagas and efforts, though unsuccessful, to change the orthography in this direction as well (p. 80).

It was during the height of the independence movement in the latter part of the nineteenth century, when Icelanders made the greatest efforts to fortify loyalty to the Icelandic linguistic heritage and to "purify" the Icelandic language, that emigration began. Historical accounts written in North America about the Danish rule in Iceland make frequent reference to the cruelty Icelanders, with their "noble and ancient language and culture," were subjected to by the colonial powers in a manner not seen in Icelandic history books. Emigration histories show that loyalty to the language and culture was no less fervent among those who left for America. The following stipulations regarding the Icelanders, agreed to by Canadian officials in 1873, demonstrates this loyalty:

(1) They were to enjoy full liberty and right of citizenship, having fulfilled residence requirements, forthwith and on the same terms as native born citizens.

(2) They were to receive a sufficiently large and suitable tract of land for a colony.

(3) They were to preserve unhindered their personal rights and their language and their nationality, for themselves and their descendants, for all time. (Kristjansson 1965, p. 18)

LITERACY

Another important factor characteristic of Icelanders and their culture is their relatively high level of literacy and the importance of the written word. If the Icelandic language expresses Icelandic culture, then only through reading the language can access be gained to the written accounts that depict the golden age of the Sagas from which the Icelandic people drew their models and heroes (Gísli Pálsson 1989; Matthiasson 1988). Reading was the favourite pastime, and shared reading, where people took turns reading while others worked, was upheld long after the migrations to North America. Throughout Iceland's history, education took place in the home, overseen by the clergy. Children could not be confirmed into the church unless they were able to read the Scriptures. As a result, while some Icelanders were not confirmed until young adulthood, the reading requirement secured a relatively high literacy level through the centuries (exactly how high may be a matter of dispute). According to immigration historians, the penniless peasants who came to North America were thus generally literate and well versed in the Sagas and various religious doctrines, as well as able to recite and often create poetry for their own and others' enjoyment. Letter writing back home was frequent. Officials who travelled in Iceland to recruit settlers commented on how well the Icelanders were informed of the conditions of those who went before them. It was noted when the first Icelandic settlers came to Winnipeg that their suitcases were heavy not with tools or clothing, but with books (Þorsteinn Þ. Þorsteinsson 1940).

The tradition of literacy continued in North America. Although Icelanders in North America recognized immediately the need for formal education, especially in English, they continued to teach their children how to read and write in Icelandic. The majority of the informants in this study stated that they could speak, read, and write Icelandic before they started elementary school.

THE LINGUISTIC HOMOGENEITY OF ICELANDIC

The discussion of Icelandic dialects has been characterized by a controversy as to what constitutes a dialect and whether any dialects exist in Icelandic at all. Hreinn Benediktsson (1959a) suggests two reasons for this controversy. The first reason is the fact that two people from any part of the country can converse without the slightest difficulty. The other reason, Benediktsson contends, is the "general opinion of most Icelanders that, from an historical point of view, Icelandic is a co ntinuous, indivisible whole, which has not undergone any noticeable changes since the period of literary flowering in Iceland in t he Middle Ages" (p. 72). Today there is a co nsensus among linguists, supported by several studies, that different features exist t hat, although minimal, distinguish different regional dialects in I celandic from one another (Björn Guðfinnsson 1946, 1964; H öskuldur Þráinsson 1985; Kristján Árnason 1987; and others). The minimal linguistic differences found among different regional varieties of Icelandic contrasts with the vast dialectal differences found in the languages closest to Icelandic, Faeroese and Norwegian. The issue whether social variation exists in I celandic is still being debated, although it seems counterintuitive to assume that Icelandic, contrary to what is found generally among the languages of the world, is not socially stratified. Some indications of the social stratification of language are beginning to surface in studies by younger linguists (see Ásta Svavarsdóttir et al. 1984; and Sigríður Sigurjónsdóttir and Joan Maling 2001). We have no way of knowing the extent to which social variation existed in I celandic at the time of the emigrations and thus we have no information about social variation in the speech of the Icelandic emigrants to North America.

Scholars disagree on the causes for the relative uniformity of Icelandic. Many contend that the prevailing purism and general desire to preserve the Old Icelandic language of the Sagas helped to minimize linguistic differences between regions. Helgi Guðmundsson (1977, in G ísli Pálsson 1989, p. 1) suggests several external reasons that prevented major diffusion of Icelandic according to region. Helgi Guðmundsson writes that during the settlement of Iceland, the settlers mixed several Scandinavian dialects into a unified language—the implication being that this mixing was prompted by the shift of loyalty to what they saw as a n Icelandic language. Second, Helgi

Guðmundsson believes that communications within the country were relatively easy. He suggests that labourers and vagrants travelled regularly from one farm to another, so few regions were permanently isolated. Finally, Denmark's language policy in Iceland during its colonial rule seems to have been weak or non-existent.

Milroy and Milroy (1985) also provide a convincing argument attributing the lack of variation to "the practical importance attached to maintaining strongly established kin and friendship networks" (p. 377). This will be discussed further in the next chapter.

Added to this list of reasons for the homogeneity of Icelandic is the overlooked importance of the church and the clergy, who oversaw education. The local clergyman prepared all children in Iceland for confirmation and the clergy were mostly educated at the Latin School in Iceland, a bastion of language purism (Halldór Halldórsson 1979). The Bible was translated into Icelandic as early as 1584 and sermons in the churches were always given in Icelandic. Since most Icelandic ministers got their education at the Latin School, ministers also tended to be guardians of the mother tongue. Jón Bjarnason, the religious and secular leader of the Icelanders in North America during the early years of settlement, came out of this mould. There are several written accounts of Jón Bjarnason's fervour, not only in preserving Icelandic in Canada, but also in preserving the autonomy of the Icelandic colony. Jón Bjarnason rejected financial assistance to the Icelandic settlers from the Norwegian Lutheran Synod in America on the grounds that Icelanders had left America to be free of "foreign rule" (Kristjansson 1965).

Linguistic Variation in Icelandic

While it is true that Icelandic has been relatively uniform diachronically and synchronically, there do exist phonological features that identify a speaker with a certain geographical region in Iceland. And although these differences are not as pronounced as they used to be, certainly, during the time of the emigrations, these were identifiable. As the focus of this study is the description of North American Icelandic, in general, and vowel mergers, which were features of certain regional and perhaps social dialects in Iceland, in particular, a sketch of the features that separate the different regional varieties found in Icelandic in Iceland is in order. This description is based on extensive studies of dialect features in Icelandic in the 1940s conducted by Björn Guðfinnsson (1946, 1964, 1981). This study was chosen because it is the closest study in time to the period when the emigrants left Iceland. Björn Guðfinnsson's study involved 10,000 informants, including 7000 children or 93% of all children in Iceland between the ages of ten and thirteen. These studies were conducted some sixty-five years after the emigrations to America started and some thirty-five years after they ended. All features are known to have been well established by the time of the emigrations.

Björn Guðfinnsson identified eight variant feature groups that may be considered contrastive in different varieties of Icelandic (1981, p. 22). It should be added that the boundaries between the variants are not clear, so that on both sides of the dialect region where a variant is general in the speech of the informants, there are areas where the variant appears some of the time in the speech of some informants.

In terms of transcription, the distinction between p and b, t and d, k and g in Icelandic orthography is that of aspiration. No voiced stops exist in Icelandic. Here IPA transcription is used for non-aspirated /p, t, k/ (b, d, g in Icelandic orthography), and /ph, th, kh/ are aspirated stops (p, t, k in Icelandic orthography).

1. *Harðmæli-linmæli*

Harðmæli 'hard pronunciation' refers to aspiration of stops following long vowels typical of the north and northeast of Iceland. Accordingly, words like *tapa* 'to lose' are pronounced [thapha], *aka* 'to drive' as [akha], and *sækja* 'fetch' as [saikhja] as opposed to [thapa], [aka] and [saikja] as used in other areas of the country and known as linmæli. Both these features were well established before the emigration period.

2. *Voicing of sonorants before (p, t, k)*

Voicing of sonorants before (p, t, k) is another feature characteristic of speech in the northern part of Iceland, in Eyjafjörður, and, to a lesser degree, in northern and southern Þingeyjarsýsla, and in Skagafjörður. Thus, words like *lampi* 'lamp' are pronounced [lamphi], *stúlka* 'girl' is pronounced [stulkha], and *menntun* [mEnthYn] rather than [lampi], [stulka], and [mEntYn], as said (typical) elsewhere in Iceland. Devoicing of sonorants before (p, t, k) is believed to be a more recent feature. However, both are old features of the language.

3. *(hv) vs. (kv) pronunciation*

In southeastern Icelandic, words beginning with hv- are pronounced as a voiceless fricative [x] in words like *hvalur* 'whale' and *hvítur* 'white', while other dialects have (kv) [khvalYR], [khvituR]. (kv) is considered the more recent feature and was widely documented by the mid-1800s. This distinction is disappearing.

4. *Pronunciation of (-ngl) vs. (-ŋl)*

In some regions of northern Iceland, words like *hringla* 'rattle' are pronounced [hRiŋkla] versus the more widespread [hRiŋla]. This feature is found only in the speech of few older speakers in some remote parts of northern Iceland. Kristján Árnason (1987, p. 91) comments that this is not a very salient or marked feature.

5. *Pronunciation of (r) + (n) or (l) as (rn) or (rl)*

In the eastern part of Iceland, in and around Austur Skaftafellssýsla, the word *varla* 'hardly' is pronounced as [vaRla], and *stjarna* 'star' as [styaRna], whereas in other parts of the country, these types of words are pronounced with a voiceless /R/ and /l/ as in [vaR̥ l̥a] or [val̥a] and [stjaR̥na] or [stjan̥a]. The [vaRla] pronunciation is older.

6. *(a + ŋg) vs. (au + ŋg)*

Speech in the far western part of Iceland is characterized by a monophthongal pronunciation of vowels before a velar nasal and velar stop. Thus words like *langur* 'long' (masc.), *löng* 'long' (fem.), and *hanki* 'hook' are pronounced as [laŋkuR], [löŋk], and [haŋki], whereas the diphthongal form is more widespread [lauŋkuR], [löyŋk], [hauŋki]. Very recently, this feature seems to be reappearing in the speech of some Icelanders. This is probably an affectation and an effort to identify oneself with this area.

7. (o:yI) and (I:yi) vs. (oiyI) and (iyI)

Another monophthongal form unrelated to the one discussed above appears in southeastern Icelandic before the cluster glide [y] + [I]: *bogi* 'bow' *stigi* 'ladder' is pronounced [bo:yI] and [stI:yi] instead of the more common [boiyI] and [stiyI].

8. Réttmæli-Flámæli

In three areas of Iceland, in the southwest, east, and, to a lesser extent, in the northwest, speech was characterized by the apparent mergers of long [I:] and [E:], on the one hand, and long [Y:] and [ö:], on the other. Subsequently, words like *sigur* [sI:γYR] 'victory', *hugur* [hY:γYR] 'mind', *vefa* [vE:va] 'weave', and *tölur* [tö:lYR] 'numbers' sound like [sE:γYR], [hö:γYR], [vI:va], and [tY:lYR]. This results in words like *viður* 'wood' and *veður* 'weather' becoming homophonous, and *flugur* 'flies' becomes homophonous with *flögur* 'chips'. Both variants are fairly recent in that they grew out of other vowel changes that took place in earlier forms of Icelandic. The apparent mergers are referred to as Flámæli 'skewed speech', while the non-merging varieties are referred to as Réttmæli 'correct speech'. Although not mentioned in the Björn Guðfinnsson study, this variety may have carried a further social stigma.

FIGURE 1

The Distribution of Flámæli in Iceland in the 1940s

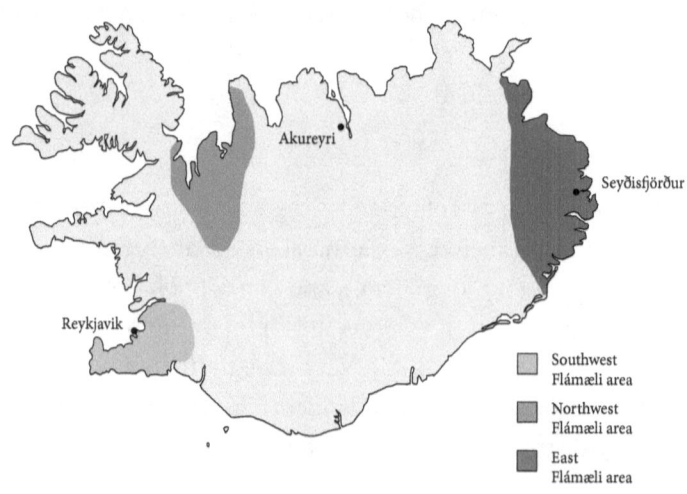

Flámæli is a characteristic feature of North American Icelandic and is the subject of our study. Figure 1 illustrates Flámæli's distribution in Iceland in the 1940s.

EMIGRATION

The timing of the emigrations may have aided in the preservation of Icelandic in North America. Emigration from Iceland to America started in the 1870s, late in the context of European emigration, and continued until the First World War. The majority of Icelanders arrived in North America between 1875 and 1890. According to the census of 1890, there were 70,240 people living in Iceland (Þorsteinn Þ. Þorsteinsson 1940, p. 144), down from about 72,442 counted a decade earlier in 1880 (Þorsteinn Þ. Þorsteinsson 1945, p. 112). Sources disagree as to how many Icelanders actually settled in North America. Júníus Kristjánsson (1983, Table 1) gives the number 14,268 but there may be thousands more. Gerrard (1985) claims that close to 20,000 Icelanders emigrated but he does not identify his sources (p. 6). These numbers suggest that almost a quarter of the population of Iceland left the country.

Three main factors motivated emigration from Iceland. First, in the eighteenth and nineteenth centuries, Iceland was devastated by natural disasters: extreme weather conditions with accompanying ice; epidemic diseases; and a series of volcanic eruptions that spewed poisonous gas over populous regions in the north and east, killing livestock and taking its toll on the already fragile land. This series of disasters came on top of hardship and poverty that had prevailed through the centuries. The general population decreased and the numbers of destitute people grew. This increased the financial burden on those farmers left with any resources, who were obliged under Icelandic law to provide for the poor. Many unfortunates became virtual serfs at the mercy of their communities and the farmers who were charged with their support. Families were separated. Young people were forbidden to marry unless they could support themselves and most could not. It was simply more economical for counties (*hreppar*) to ship families off to America rather than support them at home. Some were disillusioned and no longer believed that a tolerable life could ever be lived in Iceland and still others simply went looking for better opportunities for themselves and their families. Böðvar Guðmundsson's books depict, in a vi vid and historically accurate manner, the trials and tribulations of an Icelandic immigrant family deported to North America (Böðvar Guðmundsson 1995, 1996).

The second factor encouraging emigration was the general awakening in Europe at the time to the rights of individuals and to civil liberties. This awakening had found support in Iceland, resulting in an effort to regain independence from Denmark. In 1874 Iceland became self-governing in domestic affairs and conditions began to improve. The fight for independence and for civil liberties sparked hope in the minds of the thousands of poverty-stricken Icelanders who saw an opportunity to escape to a better life.

At the same time Canadian and American officials, prompted by the opening up of vast western and northern territories in North America for settlement, were actively recruiting immigrants in Iceland. For the disillusioned, this third factor seemed to offer an alternative to their demise.

These factors led to emigration of Icelanders in search of a better life in North America. It is important to note again that although disillusioned with their old homeland, these immigrants left with the intention of creating a new homeland, as a group, in the new country. They wanted a new Iceland, where they could stay together, preserve their own culture and language, and improve the material quality of their lives (Þorsteinn Þ. Þorsteinsson 1940, p. 157; Gerrard 1985, p. 19).

Although most regions in Iceland saw an exodus of some of its inhabitants, many parishes in the north and northeast, which were hardest hit by natural disasters, saw most of their inhabitants emigrate. Table 2 illustrates the number of emigrants from each *sýsla* or region in Iceland from 1870 to 1914.

NEW ICELAND

In the New World, the Icelandic immigrants sought a tract of land that would be uninhabited and large enough to eventually accommodate all Icelanders. The colony would be open for settlement only to Icelanders (Kristjansson 1965, p. 21). Scouts were dispersed to survey various regions of the northern United States and Alaska for appropriate sites for settlement. Two attempts at

TABLE 2

Numbers of Emigrants from Iceland to North America

Region	Number
North Múlasýsla	2738
South Múlasýsla	1057
Skaftafellssýslur	269
Rangárvallasýsla	116
Vestmannaeyjar	297
Árnessýsla	368
Gullbringu-og Kjósarsýslur	297
Reykjavík	294
Borgarfjarðarsýsla	299
Mýrarsýsla	556
Snæfells-og Hnappadalssýslur	496
Dalasýsla	436
Barðastrandarsýsla	205
Ísafjarðarsýsla	435
Strandasýsla	171
Húnavatnssýsla	1361
Skagafjarðarsýsla	1422
Eyjafjarðarsýsla	1024
Þingeyjarsýsla	1945
Residence unknown	482
Total number of emigrants	14,268

(Source: Júníus Kristjánsson 1983, Table 1)

settlement in Michigan and eastern Canada were abandoned, and efforts to move all Icelanders to Alaska never materialized despite US President Grant's encouragement. It is testimony to the Icelandic spirit that Jón Ólafsson, one of the explorers sent to Alaska, wrote in his report after an expedition to survey land for settlement by Icelanders that Alaska was

> eminently suitable for the Icelandic people and in Alaska they would be independent and free, and Icelandic could be made the prevailing language. He envisaged the possibility of ten thousand settlers in fifteen years, and that with the population doubling in numbers every twenty-

five years; the settlement would ultimately extend from the Pacific Ocean to Hudson Bay. (Paraphrased by Kristjansson 1965, pp. 21–22)

Icelanders have never been much for thinking small. Needless to say, Jón Ólafsson's dream never materialized.

Finally, land was made available to the Icelanders by the Canadian government in what was then part of the North-West Territories on the shores of Lake Winnipeg, just north of the Province of Manitoba. There may have been political reasons for the Canadian government's offer of this particular land that also may account for the leniency they showed towards the Icelanders' efforts at autonomy. According to Matthiasson (1988), this part of the North-West Territories was mostly inhabited by First Nations people and especially Métis who were descendants of French fur traders and Aboriginal women. Because the region had a "bad reputation" due to conflicts with the Métis and the inhospitableness of the land, the government had had no success in recruiting Anglo-Saxon settlers. The anglophone government did not wish to add to the influence of the French by allowing French speakers to settle in areas already dominated by the French-speaking Métis. The Canadian government thus looked to eastern Europe and Iceland to recruit settlers (Matthiasson 1988, p. 5).

This site was deemed appropriate for Icelanders due to the abundance of timber for housing, good soil for farming, and ample fishing prospects in the lake (Gerrard 1985, p. 22). The surveyors were guided by the fact that emigrating Icelanders were used to "mixed" farming and fishing and would therefore fare better closer to the lake (Kristjansson 1965, p. 23). One of the informants in this study, a well-to-do farmer, remarked that it was ironic that the Icelanders passed over more fertile lands to the south, later settled by Mennonites and others, to settle in the overgrown wetlands of the Interlake region where farming was almost impossible until the arrival of large farming equipment.

New Iceland was founded on October 21, 1875. Icelanders were the only ethnic group in the region afforded autonomy in their own affairs. The colony extended north from the boundary of Manitoba up by the shores of Lake Winnipeg in what was then called the North-West Territories. (Canadian Icelanders refer to the settlement as the "colony.") This site was "reserved for

Icelanders alone" (Gerrard 1985, p. 23). Several accounts are found of how Aboriginal peoples helped the Icelanders fish and farm in the unfamiliar terrain. Gerrard (1985) suggests that there arose some initial dispute about the settlement from the indigenous Aboriginal and Métis populations, but doesn't elaborate.

The Icelandic settlers lost no time in o rganizing their new homeland. Due to delays in establishing a government for the District of Keewatin, into which New Iceland was to be incorporated, the new arrivals were without ties to a provincial or district government for some time. The Icelanders subsequently set up their own government in t he colony based on the Icelandic Alþing (parliament).

On January 4th, 1876, the colony's first council meeting, with five annually elected officials, was held. The responsibility of the council, or þingráð, was to ensure an equitable distribution of the supplies provided by the government, supervision of sanitation and health, and fire protection (Kristjansson 1965, p. 37). All permanent residents of the colony over twenty-one years of age who possessed an "unblemished" character were eligible to vote. This included women, a progressive notion for those times. The articles of the constitution of the colony were subject to amendment at a general meeting of the voters in the colony (Kristansson 1965, p. 57). Laws for the colony were written in Icelandic, and, from 1878 to 1887, New Iceland was a republic in theory (Ruth 1964) and a democracy in reality, with its own laws, education, and religion. The English language was, for the most part, absent from the colony for the first decade, except in education.

The colony's legislative body was na med *Vatnsþing* 'Lakething' (*þing* means 'meeting' or 'parliament'). Four *byggðir* 'settlements' made up the þing. These were given Icelandic names, which still exist: *Víðinesbyggð, Árnesbyggð, Fljótsbyggð,* and *Mikleyjarbyggð*. Icelandic was the official language of the colony except in the school, and it was declared that no one other than Icelanders would be allowed to settle in the area so that the language and heritage could be preserved as long as possible (Þorsteinn Þ. Þorsteinsson 1940, p. 111). The words of Jón Bjarnason, the religious leader of the colony, embody this view:

það væri heilög og háleit skylda hvers Íslendings að gleyma ekki eigin tungu sinni né held ur blanda hana alls konar hrafnamáli. [It is the sacred duty of every Icelander neither to forget their own language nor to mix into it some kind of slang.] (Þorsteinn Þ. Þorsteinsson 1943, p. 234) [author's translation].

The first two years in New Iceland were characterized by the severe and unfamiliar weather, the settlers' being unaccustomed to hunting and fishing in the frozen lake, a smallpox epidemic, and, by the first spring, severe floods. Politically, a division occurred in the colony between the followers of two fiery young ministers of the church. One was Jón Bjarnason, an Icelandic Lutheran minister; the other was Páll Þorláksson, who had been educated at a Norwegian Unitarian seminary. Páll Þorláksson offered financial assistance to the settlers from the Norwegian Unitarian Synod (Kristjansson 1965; Jónas Þór 1980). Both men were educated at Iceland's Latin school and both were dedicated "preservationists." Jón Bjarnason and his men felt that the Unitarian church represented by Páll Þorláksson was too foreign and literal in its interpretation of the Bible. Furthermore, they had left Iceland in order not to take charity from foreigners. This division is important to our study, for the two factions each published their own newspapers, which promoted the rhetoric put forth by each group and were followed eagerly by Icelanders in Canada and North Dakota. This division continued along political lines later on and appears to have contributed much to preserving interest in reading and writing and eventually retaining Icelandic.

As a result of the floods and the political/religious divisions, many of the original settlers in New Iceland dispersed to two other main settlements. Some went to Vatnabyggð, around the town of Wynyard, halfway between Regina and Saskatoon in Saskatchewan. Others followed the Reverend Páll Þorláksson to settle around Mountain in Pembina County, North Dakota, in the United States. Still others settled in Winnipeg in search of secure employment. As immigration from Iceland continued, the primary destination of most Icelanders continued to be New Iceland, although many later scattered throughout Canada and the United States. New Iceland, on the other hand, remains the centre for Icelandic culture and heritage in North America, although many of the institutions organized to preserve Icelandic language and culture are situated in Winnipeg.

In the early years New Iceland was mostly rural. Each homestead was given a name, according to Icelandic custom. Most of the initial homesteads were situated along Lake Winnipeg, so that fish could be caught for food. Many stories are told of the unfamiliarity of the Icelandic farmers with planting, hunting, and fishing through ice. Soon small towns began forming. Gimli, on Lake Winnipeg by the mouth of the Icelandic River, became the centre for commerce and transportation. Later, the towns of Riverton and Arborg grew and gradually farming was begun inland from the lake.

Social life in the colony was always lively. For the first decade of "self rule," frequent meetings were held to discuss the government of the colony. Each member of the council was responsible for holding meetings at home to inform his constituents of the latest developments. There were annual productions of Icelandic plays (this tradition continues today, except the plays are presented in English), choral societies flourished, and poetry reading was a popular pastime.

The colony was isolated from the outside world for many years. The first road into the colony was built as early as 1877, but wet ground and mud made this road impassable most of the year. Travel to the nearest cities, Selkirk or Winnipeg, was by boat in summer and on ice in winter. The isolation was not broken until the laying of the railroad some thirty years after the founding of the colony.

Travel to and from Iceland was almost non-existent from 1914 until 1975, with the exceptions of "official" visits back and forth. In 1975 regular excursion flights began between Winnipeg and Iceland and visits became more frequent. Despite the physical isolation, the New Icelanders kept abreast of current events in Iceland and elsewhere through their Icelandic newspapers and extensive letter writing.

The isolation and concentration of Icelanders in the Canadian settlements meant that integration into a Canadian mainstream society came slowly, especially in Canada's New Iceland. The immediate neighbours of New Iceland were Ukrainians to the west and Mennonites and Doukhobors from Russia to the south and west. Winnipeg eventually became ethnically diverse with eastern Europeans, Germans, and other populations joining the existing French, Scots, and English.

There is very little indication that Icelanders met with serious obstacles in their efforts to take advantage of the opportunities afforded them by the larger society. In Winnipeg, "Icelanders found a relatively high position" in the hierarchy of ethnic groups represented there (Matthiasson 1988, p. 8). Icelanders lived in their own neighbourhood, "the West End," where they had their own shops and schools. The medium of instruction was English but many of the teachers were Icelandic. Yet, the Icelanders had social mobility and, very early, had representatives in education, politics, business, and medicine. Matthiasson (1988) puts forth several explanations for this mobility. First, there were no stereotypes of Icelanders present prior to their coming, and they had been given a favourable introduction by Lord Dufferin, the Governor General of Canada, who had visited Iceland (Kristjansson 1965). It also worked to their advantage that the Icelanders were among the first to settle the region. In Winnipeg, many Icelanders prospered during the early period of expansion from a small frontier town to a bustling city and were able to take advantage of the subsequent boom in real estate. In New Iceland, many of the already established Icelandic farmers hired later immigrants to the area, who in turn often learned Icelandic in the process. Foreigners learning Icelandic and the misunderstandings that ensue from this are a running theme in humorous storytelling in the North American Icelandic community. It serves to underscore the tight connection Icelanders see between their identity and their language that it is a curiosity when others learn and use the language as a foreign language.

Early literacy may have aided the original immigrants' children, who found their ways to institutions of higher education. Icelanders also quickly aligned themselves with Scots and English and avoided the label "ethnic." Marriage outside the group was not common in the early years, but when it did occur, it was more likely to be to Protestant Scots or English who were called *hérlendir menn* or 'people from here' rather than to Catholic or Jewish eastern Europeans or people of other ethnic origins.

It seems clear that if Icelanders experienced prejudice (and some did, according to informants), it did not affect the view they had of themselves and thus did little to prevent them from assimilating.

LIVING IN TWO CULTURES

While Icelanders in Winnipeg had access to upward mobility, they did not reject their Icelandic ethnicity. Many had one identity for the outside world and another for the inside group. Bilingualism and biculturalism came easily to them. They saw an advantage in Anglicizing their names; some were known to change names according to the company they kept, retaining their Icelandic names among Icelanders but using English names outside their closest network. Being bilingual and bicultural has served Icelanders well. Even though Icelanders integrated quickly, taking part in government, education, and commerce from the outset, integration did not seem to interfere with their wish to retain their old customs and own culture and language. This duality (see also Matthiasson 1988) may be a trait that Icelanders brought with them after centuries of dominance by Denmark, which ultimately did not have much lasting effect on the Icelandic culture or language, especially in comparison to the effect Danish had on Norwegian or English had on Gaelic. This attitude is also reminiscent of the time in the year 1000 when Icelanders agreed to officially become Christians but at home nonetheless continued to worship their old pagan gods.

The description above does not pertain to all descendants of the Icelandic settlers. Although bilingualism was the norm, especially in the rural settlements, some settlers assimilated quickly into the mainstream culture.

Today, descendants of Icelandic immigrants in North America are, for the most part, integrated into Canadian or American society. The West End in Winnipeg is no longer an Icelandic neighbourhood, and even the Icelandic towns in New Iceland have large populations of other ethnic backgrounds. The Icelandic newspaper *Lögberg-Heimskringla* is written entirely in English and so is *The Icelandic-Canadian* magazine, although the content of both is concerned with Icelandic themes (Matthiasson 1988). Icelandic Canadians and Icelandic Americans are prominent in all areas of Canadian and American life from the arts and filmmaking to business, politics, and academia.

However, current efforts in Canada to encourage ethnic consciousness have also enhanced an interest in things Icelandic. Today Gimli is the site of Íslendingadagurinn [Icelanders' Day], the largest annual Icelandic festival in North America. There is a flourishing exchange program between Iceland and Manitoba with regular visits back and forth, and, since 1975, Icelandic theatre groups, choirs, novelists, and politicians have been frequent visitors to the Icelandic settlements in North America. Iceland now has an official consulate in Winnipeg.

CONCLUSION

Several factors have influenced the retention of Icelandic in North America. The first is the association in the minds of Icelanders between the language and their culture, which fostered a loyalty to the language. The second factor is the high level of literacy and the importance placed on literary activities in the home. Third, the initial geographic isolation leading to the establishment of a self-governing "Icelandic community" with its own Icelandic forms of government and constitution helped to conserve the language. The final factor is the ease with which the Icelandic settlers became bilingual and bicultural. This is often found among ethnic groups with a strong ethnic identity and is seen as aiding preservation, in this case, of the Icelandic language beyond the traditional three-generation stage that spans the survival of most immigrant languages in North America.

The early settlers wanted to create a New Iceland where Icelandic culture and language would dominate. They soon saw the greater opportunities afforded to them by the larger society and were able to take advantage of those opportunities without detriment to their loyalty to their roots. Bilingualism and biculturalism were comfortable to them. Today's North American Icelanders express their Icelandic background through their more dominant North American identity. Perhaps the clearest sign of assimilation's having been completed is the overt efforts to enhance one's Icelandic ethnicity without seeing oneself as an Icelander but as a Canadian or an American.

CHAPTER 2 **THE LIFE CYCLE OF NORTH AMERICAN ICELANDIC**

In this chapter, I place the socio-historical context of North American Icelandic within the larger theoretical discussion of language retention and regression in bilingual communities, and of bilingual individuals and their transition to a second culture. I revisit the discussion about the forces that served to preserve Icelandic in North America, especially the view that Icelandic has survived longer than the two to three generations proposed by linguists as the life span of most immigrant languages (Ferguson 1959). These forces are: the central role of the language in Icelandic culture and identity, along with a high level of literacy and literary activity; the tightly knit, isolated immigrant communities; and a pragmatic attitude towards bilingualism and biculturalism.

In the second half of the chapter, I discuss the forces that will lead to the language variety's eventual attrition: the close and intense contact with English; the narrowing functional range of Icelandic; and the disintegration of formerly tight-knit social networks. All these factors will cause North American Icelandic to suffer the fate of most immigrant languages in North

America and die out. The data on NA Icelandic, collected in 1986, show clear evidence of language regression due to direct transfer from English, but also due to simplification processes that result from the reduced functionality of Icelandic as English takes over as the dominant language of Americans and Canadians of Icelandic extraction.

THEORETICAL ORIENTATION

For proper understanding of language as a medium of expression, we must study linguistic behaviour within the context of the norms and traditions laid down by the speech community. Living languages do not exist in a vacuum. Languages survive because they are used by people and they reflect the realities of those speakers. Language varieties change as the speakers' realities change and can diverge and split into mutually unintelligible languages due to geographical or social distance and different social contexts. The evolution of the Indo-European family of languages, from Proto-Indo-European to present-day European languages, is the most-studied example of this phenomenon.

The most dramatic language change is often seen in situations where two or more languages come into contact. This is true for the case reported here, when an immigrant language has coexisted for two or more generations with the host language. The study of North American Icelandic in the context of language attrition or language death is especially interesting because it gives us a unique opportunity to study how an isolated and conservative language in its home country, itself under attack by English, fares in an intense language contact situation. It gives us a chance to study accelerated language change in progress—accelerated due to the narrowing functional range of an immigrant language as the host language takes over more and more domains of language use. The host language is used for all speech events outside the home, and use of the immigrant language is confined to the home and family. When the forces that sustain fully fledged national languages, the forces that work against change, are no longer available, languages become more susceptible to change and the rate of change in progress is accelerated (for a closer look, see the discussion of Flámæli in chapters 5 to 7).

North American Icelandic is in the final stages of attrition. It is spoken by bilingual people who, during the time of this study in 1986, used it almost entirely in the most familiar and intimate situations at home and with family and friends. They used English on all other occasions. From the end of immigration in 1914 u p until 1975, t here was li ttle communication between Iceland and the Icelandic immigrants in North America, with the exception of the exchange of letters. A small minority of people of Icelandic descent in North America still speak Icelandic and probably only a h andful have Icelandic as their primary language. The majority of informants in 1986 were over fifty years of age. Within one or two generations, NA Icelandic will have followed other immigrant languages in North America into obscurity.

THE INCEPTION AND DEVELOPMENT OF NORTH AMERICAN ICELANDIC

The results of this study indicate that the grammar and lexicon of Icelandic in North America developed its own characteristics once applied to the realities in the new world, but show evidence of language internal changes as well as changes due to transfer from English that are consistent with what we know about language regression and attrition. A description of these changes is found in Chapter 5. F rom the beginning of the last century until today, modern Icelandic, a na tional language supported by a str ong purist tradition, has undergone only minor changes. Each variety has changed in different ways; these changes are most apparent within their lexicons, as different words are created or borrowed into each variety to serve the same function. To paraphrase Sapir's words (1921, p. 193), the loanwords in both varieties constitute an interesting commentary on the different histories of the two Icelandic cultures. In the case of North American Icelandic, the language soon began to develop lexical items for concepts and items that reflected the realities of the immigrants' new life (see Chapter 3). However, strong mechanisms remained in place to ensure the survival of Icelandic in Amer ica. Characteristics and cultural quirks of the speech community, seen in t he strong connection between the language and the identity of the speakers, as well as in their comfort with the duality of a bilingual existence, served to preserve the language. So did the historical contexts such as the timing of the emigration and the unique history of the Icelandic settlements in Manitoba and in North Dakota.

LANGUAGE, CULTURE, AND IDENTITY

From the very beginning of Icelandic settlement in North America, there were organized efforts to retain Icelandic. The charter that designated the Interlake region of Manitoba to the Icelanders stipulated that "[T]hey were to preserve unhindered their personal rights and their language and their nationality, for themselves and their descendants" (Kristjansson 1965). Jón Bjarnason, the religious and secular leader of the Icelandic immigrants, was a fervent language purist and fought for the establishment of organized efforts to ensure the survival of Icelandic culture in North America (Ruth 1964). He called it a "sacred duty" to preserve the language (Þorsteinn Þ. Þorsteinsson 1943). Saturday schools for Icelandic were formed and held from 1885 to 1912. In 1909 Reverend Jón Bjarnason complained that Icelandic youths had such limited Icelandic that it was hampering the Confirmation preparations that had continued to be conducted in Icelandic. In 1913 the Icelandic community established the Jón Bjarnason Academy. The Manitoba Department of Education offered Icelandic as a second language on the program of studies at Wesley College (now the University of Manitoba) and at Gimli from 1901 until 1951 (Ruth 1964, p. 25). From 1919 to 1933, travelling teachers went from farm to farm and town to town to instruct children in Icelandic.

In 1920 a library of Icelandic books was founded. In 1936, through a donation of a private library of Icelandic books to the University of Manitoba, the Icelandic Collection was founded. Three years later, in 1939, the collection was designated as an official depository of Icelandic publications. The library was redesignated in 1978 and in 2002 a special library facility, specifically designed for the Icelandic Collection, was dedicated at the University of Manitoba. The collection is the major resource centre in Canada for scholars interested in Icelandic and Icelandic-Canadian studies and it serves the intellectual needs of the Icelandic community in Canada.

Although the idea had been discussed as early as 1905, interest in endowing a Chair in Icelandic at the University of Manitoba was refuelled in 1932. Due to generous individual donations to the university in 1944 and 1945 by members of the Icelandic immigrant community, an Icelandic Chair and a Department of Icelandic were established at the University of Manitoba in

1951. They were partially funded by Icelandic Canadians and partially by the Icelandic government. Another faculty position, this one in Icelandic-Canadian Studies, was designated in 1992. The University of Manitoba and the University of Iceland cosponsor annual conferences on issues of common interest.

In 1919 the Icelandic National League (INL) was formed, partly to "work for the preservation of the Icelandic language and literature in America" (Ruth 1964, p. 47). However, voices were raised early stating that any effort to preserve the language in Canada was futile. At many meetings of the league in the thirties, preservation was debated and finally a resolution accepted that "Icelandic culture could be passed on to future generations through the use of the English language to express Icelandic ideas" (Ruth 1964, p. 47). The English language magazine *The Icelandic-Canadian*, which still enjoys popularity in the Icelandic settlements, echoed this view. It is interesting to note that the Icelandic National League's membership has grown by leaps and bounds for the last decade or so. The INL's annual convention has grown from a handful of participants a decade ago to over 2000 in 2003 (Sigrid Johnson, former president of the INL, personal communication).

Icelanders also brought with them to North America the traditions of chronicling their experiences, which certainly served to preserve the language. These traditions manifested in the numerous historical documentations on the immigrants' life in the new country. Several books on the history of immigration of Icelanders in North America are available, as well as a wealth of biographies, histories of individual settlements, annual almanacs, newspapers, magazines, several historical and fictitious novels, and an abundance of poetry depicting the existence of Icelanders during their more than 125 years in North America. For this study, I had access to five volumes of genealogies of almost every family of Icelandic extraction in North America. Genealogical studies seem to be an Icelandic pastime that found its way to the new world as well. The numerous historical publications give a detailed account of everything from the everyday life of individuals to historical events that affected North American Icelanders as a group. In much the same way as their ancestors had documented the settlement of Iceland from Norway in the ninth century, the North American Icelanders chronicled their own resettlement. The number of original Icelandic works published in Canada from circa 1900 to 1961 (Salus 1971, p. 241) is: forty-one volumes of poetry, twenty-two novels or collections of stories, thirty-five volumes of histories, biographies, etc., and ten dramas. This does not include the many publications that appeared before 1900, nor the wealth of translations into Icelandic that were produced in North America. Nor does it include the numerous published newspapers, magazines, and pamphlets. This is a formidable list for an audience numbering, at best, fewer than 40,000.

In order for a publishing business this prolific to flourish, there must have been an audience to read what was presented to them. It is safe to say that for a period of time, there were more books published in Icelandic in North America than in Iceland. By all accounts, there was indeed a general interest in Icelandic publications, which certainly served to encourage the preservation of the language among North American Icelanders.

The ability to speak, read, and write Icelandic was also maintained through home schooling. Church services and Sunday school were conducted in Icelandic for many years, both in New Iceland and in Mountain, North Dakota. Ministers were brought in from Iceland. Evening courses in Icelandic are very popular among Icelandic Canadians. Icelandic is also taught at the Riverton Elementary School in Riverton, New Iceland. Enthusiasm was high in Mountain, North Dakota, about Icelandic classes held there at the time of this study. Scholarships and exchange programs are available to youngsters who wish to study Icelandic as a heritage language.

Talking about Icelandic

During the first winter in Manitoba in 1876, a newspaper, *Nýi Þjóðólfur*, was circulated, written in longhand until a printing machine was carried out to the colony. On September 10, 1877, Prentfélag Nýja Íslands 'The New Iceland Publishing Company' was formed, and the first printed newspaper, *Framfari*, began circulation. *Lögberg* and *Heimskringla*, later published in Winnipeg but with a wider circulation in all the Icelandic settlements, continued the debate between the Lutheran Liberals and the Unitarian Conservatives. This debate fuelled interest in the Icelandic newspapers and thus in reading and writing Icelandic. These two newspapers also informed Icelandic Canadians and Icelandic Americans about world events, about Icelandic affairs, and about local affairs. Publishers of both newspapers agreed on the need to preserve Icelandic in the new world, and all their articles were written in Icelandic up until the late 1970s.

In the third issue of *Lögberg* in 1888 a wr iter commented on the state of Icelandic in Winnipeg: "að málið sé strax farið að verða býsna svipljótt" 'the language is already getting frightfully ugly' [author's translation]. In the thirty-ninth issue that same year, the editor of *Lögberg* lamented the deteriorating competence in I celandic, exemplified by referring to *Lögberg* as mas culine when any respectable Icelander knows that *Lögberg* is an 'it'. By 1901 the editor of *Heimskringla* claimed that "Íslensk tunga sé orðin að a fskræmdu máli í Ameríku" 'In America, Icelandic has b ecome a distorted language' [author's translation]. In an article published in *Dialect Notes* in 1903, V ilhjálmur Stefánsson stated that there were a f ew persons around Mountain, North Dakota, who kept their Icelandic "uncorrupted," but the majority were compelled to borrow English expressions and mix them with Icelandic (p. 355).

Icelandic Americans in North Dakota shared the cultural and linguistic background of their ethnic brethren in Canada. They looked to the cultural institutions of Winnipeg as centres for Icelandic culture, while actively maintaining their own ties to Iceland by bringing Icelandic clergymen to serve in their parish. For many years the sermons were given in Icelandic and many informants proudly claimed that they had b een 'confirmed' in I celandic, "fermdur upp á íslensku." Today, however, the sermons are given in English.

While formal education policies and institutional support helped to preserve the Icelandic language, this was aided by the home traditions of the Icelandic settlers in North America. Icelanders brought with them a general literacy and an emphasis on home education (Vilhjálmur Stefánsson 1903; Haraldur Bessason 1984a, 1984b, 1984c). Consequently, not only could many second- and third-generation Icelandic Canadians speak Icelandic as children, but could also read and write Icelandic before they had formal education. Frequent letters were written back to Iceland and between the settlements. The custom of communal reading was co ntinued and the art of putting together verses was encouraged and revered. I met two octogenarians in Saskatchewan who still telephoned each other every morning. One would begin a verse in Icelandic and the other would *botna* or complete the verse (Birna Arnbjörnsdóttir 1997). The Icelandic tradition of shared reading in the evening while people worked was continued in the New World; since *amma* 'grandmother' or *afi* 'grandfather' did not know English well enough, the reading was done in Icelandic. The retention of literacy and traditions connected to literary activity may be the single most influential factor in the preservation of Icelandic in North America. North American Icelanders realized the importance of assimilation but assimilation was not attained at the expense of the old cultural heritage. The emphasis was not on knowing English well and forgetting the old language, but on knowing both languages.

Tightly Knit Social Networks and the Timing of the Immigrations

In the early years, New Iceland was mostly rural and isolated from the outside world. Each homestead was given a name according to Icelandic custom. Soon small towns began forming and, for the first decades, these towns were mainly Icelandic and upheld the tight-knit kinship networks that characterized society back in Iceland. Icelandic was the language of business and trade. It was the language of newspapers and official documents. The geographical isolation was not broken until the laying of the railroad some thirty years after the founding of the colony. Travel to and from Iceland was almost non-existent from 1914 until 1975, with a few well-documented official visits. The isolation and concentration of Icelanders in the Canadian settlements meant that integration into a Canadian mainstream society came slowly, especially in Canada's New Iceland.

Milroy and Milroy (1985) suggest that "[t]he conservatism of Icelandic and the relative lack of variation in that language may be attributed largely to the practical importance attached to maintaining strongly established kin and friendship networks over long distances and through many generations" (p. 377). These are comments about the preservation of Icelandic in Iceland but they also apply to the North American Icelandic situation. The Icelandic immigrant communities in Manitoba were isolated and consisted of dense social networks (Milroy 1980). The isolation from Canadian mainstream society and from Iceland provided fertile ground for the creation and retention of a new variety of Icelandic: North American Icelandic.

Icelanders were the first "ethnic" settlers around Winnipeg (after the Scots, English, and French). As such, they came to some prominence and their status in the community may have elevated the status of their language as well, at least within the community. The early intentions of creating New Iceland, where all Icelanders could eventually settle to the exclusion of other ethnic groups, must also have fortified the old language and culture in the new country (Kristjansson 1965). In Winnipeg, Icelanders had their own neighbourhoods and their own educational institutions and businesses (Matthiasson 1988; Kristjansson 1965). People of Icelandic descent are in the majority in New Iceland, which is the heart of Icelandic culture in North America, and their Icelandic ethnic origins are openly displayed and advertised.

The communities in and around Mountain in North Dakota were further away from the "hub" of Icelandic culture in Canada. "Icelanders" were more integrated into an existing multi-ethnic community. There is very little outward show of Icelandic presence in North Dakota. However, there seem to have been, and still are, close networks of people of Icelandic origin in Mountain. Almost continuously, from the beginning of settlement until the 1980s, Mountain had an Icelandic minister. Many church-related activities were conducted in Icelandic up until the last few decades. My introduction to the Icelandic community in Mountain in 1986 was when I stumbled upon the monthly "Icelandic" card game and was immediately invited to play a game of Whist and engage in lively conversation in Icelandic.

Bilingualism

The last important factor in the maintenance of NA Icelandic was the ease with which Canadians and Americans of Icelandic origins adopted bilingualism and biculturalism, assimilating to, and identifying with, the host culture (especially in Winnipeg and North Dakota) while maintaining a strong Icelandic identity within the Icelandic community. Nine days after their arrival in New Iceland on October 30, 1875, and before the first house was erected, a letter was sent to the Lieutenant-Governor of Manitoba stating: "The Icelanders in the colony are desirous of having a school for their children as soon as they can put up a school house. They have a teacher with them and wish to be connected to the regular education system of Canada" (Kristjansson 1965, p. 37). By Christmas a school was organized; the language of instruction was English, as the settlers recognized the need to know English for success in the new country.

The duality in terms of how the Icelanders saw themselves vis-à-vis their external condition in Iceland seems also to have served them well in the new world (Matthiasson 1988). People thought nothing of assuming two identities—one for the larger community and another for their own Icelandic group (Matthiasson 1988).

On August 8, 1888, the editor of *Lögberg* recounts the following scenario as quoted by Haraldur Bessason (1967, p. 133):

> Most Icelandic immigrants have two sets of names, one Icelandic, and the other non-Icelandic.... Some of these men appear to have a whole repertory of names on which they can draw as circumstances require. To illustrate this point a certain man, when he has just arrived from Iceland, calls himself by the name of Sveinn Grímsson, and Sveinn Grímsson is indeed the name he will be likely to use when he is among Icelanders. But this same man has also another name, Sveinn Vestmann, which he reserves for the signing of documents. Among English speaking people, however, this man's name is neither Sveinn Grímsson nor Sveinn Vestmann. To start with he may well permit the English to call him John Anderson. However, that name is likely to acquire some distasteful flavour in the mind of its possessor and warrant a further change from John Anderson to Thomas Edison or George Byron, when the man in question moves into a new community. One Icelander has already gone as far as to list himself as Mr. Christ on a voter's list here in Winnipeg.

The linguistic history of the NA Icelanders is characterized by the same duality or paradox apparent in their settlement history. The early settlers realized the need for their children to know English. On the other hand, the need to know English did not relieve the NA Icelanders of their 'duty' to read and write Icelandic.

LIVING WITH ENGLISH, SHIFTING LOYALTIES, AND THE DECLINE OF ICELANDIC

After the initial decades of isolation, the linguistic situation in the Icelandic settlements in North America over more than a 100-year period constitutes a high-contact situation, where NA Icelandic is a minority language whose speakers have gradually shifted their loyalties towards the dominant language, English.

Maintaining balanced bilingualism is challenging in a linguistic situation where use of one of the languages is confined to the home and all other registers are taken over by the other. The first generation of immigrants is heritage-language dominant, the next one or two generations become bilingual, but the third generation is host-language dominant. This is true for North American Icelandic, although, due to factors discussed in previous sections, bilingualism may have survived longer than in most immigrant communities.

Within the generative approach to language study, language change occurs when children construct grammars different from those of their parents. The regular use of two or more languages in a community often leads to transfer of grammatical features from one language to the other. When one of the languages is almost entirely relegated to the most informal speech situations, there is an added probability that language use becomes inconsistent to the point of causing language change. Dressler (1972) found "fluctuations and uncertainties" in the speech of his Breton informants; he observed that uncertainty results in free variation, which in turn renders perception difficult. Dorian found that certain obligatory rules become optional and that certain features become sporadic (1977). Dressler agrees. He claims, "If a rule is optional with the older generation ... it is lost in the disintegrating language of the younger generation" (1972, p. 452). An example from North American Icelandic would be when parents use the verb *að langa* (want) interchangeably as an impersonal verb and say *mig langar* (I [dat.] want) or as a personal verb as in *ég langa* (I [nom.] want). Their child hears the rule inconsistently and is likely to choose the unmarked personal version in his speech. This feature, well established in North American Icelandic, then becomes an obligatory rule—i.e., is always used as an impersonal verb—thus causing changes in the way the language is used.

Variability in the speech of adult bilinguals is social as well as grammatical. The prime reason for giving up a language is an extensive functional reallocation of its domain to another language (Hyltenstam and Viberg 1993). As ethnic identities began to shift with each generation, it was inevitable that English began to play a larger role in the Icelandic immigrants' lives, and that the conditions that fortified Icelandic began to be eroded. As the functional range of the language was reduced (Hill 1978), so was its verbal repertoire and stylistic range. There are fewer occasions to speak, fewer occasions to write the language, and the range of likely topics of discussion narrows. The context or the relationship between participants in speech acts becomes limited to friends, relatives, acquaintances; i.e., the most informal registers. Changes that are characteristic of the most relaxed register, or most informal speech, become prevalent. This is the case for NA Icelandic. Children who initially grow up speaking Icelandic go to school and bring home English, the younger siblings follow, and soon the children have a life in common that is outside the realm of the language of the parents. While the parents (i.e., those who learned English) were Icelandic-dominant bilinguals, the children, in most cases, become English-dominant. As the children's centre of existence moves outside the home, English takes over, even in the most intimate speech situations. Formerly tightly knit social networks begin to disintegrate, new people move in who do not speak Icelandic, and children and grandchildren move on. There is no longer the institutional support necessary for Icelandic as a fully fledged mother tongue as English becomes the medium for transactions outside the family and with younger persons.

Linguistic purism runs deep in the Icelandic psyche and its effect should not be ignored, even though the informants in this study do not see themselves as the guardians of the mother tongue in the way that their cousins in Iceland did. Linguistic purism found its way to the NA Icelandic settlements in the form of extreme loyalty to the old language, as exemplified by the frequent newspaper articles deploring the condition of Icelandic in the "colony." North American Icelanders were avid readers of newspapers, books, and poetry written or translated into standard Icelandic. Informants seemed consciously aware they did not speak mainstream Icelandic. They frequently mentioned that they themselves did not speak 'proper' Icelandic, often followed by a suggestion that they knew people who did. Comments like the following were quite common: "hann pabbi talaði ósköp fallega íslensku" 'my father spoke beautiful Icelandic,' and "amma kunni að tala rétta íslensku" 'my grandmother knew how to speak correct Icelandic,' and even "börnin tala íslensku en eru nógu gáfuð til að tala hana ekki fyrir framan aðra" 'the children speak Icelandic but they are smart enough not to speak it in front of others'. Others commented that their way of speaking was not the same as in Iceland but that it worked for them. This is best exemplified by the following favourite quote by an informant speaking of her mother's wish never to forget how to speak Icelandic: "hún vantaði aldrei að gleyma að tala íslensku" (Birna Arnbjörnsdóttir 1994c).

I had an opportunity to take part in two social occasions in Mountain: the centennial anniversary of the first Icelandic church in North Dakota, and an "Icelandic" picnic. Very little Icelandic was spoken on either of these occasions except in groups where one or more guests from Iceland were present. One informant remarked that the only time she could think of when Icelandic was used outside the home these days was at the funeral of a prominent "Icelander," out of reverence for the deceased.

Results of an informal survey of attitudes towards Icelandic by Icelandic Americans in North Dakota in 1986 suggest a very favourable view towards all things Icelandic and a desire to know more of the language and culture. However, most of those surveyed did not think that, for pragmatic reasons, Icelandic could survive much longer in North America. A clear picture emerges of the use of Icelandic in North Dakota. Out of fifty people surveyed, thirty-two spoke Icelandic exclusively to their parents and grandparents and most often to their siblings as preschool-aged children. As adults, the same individuals speak Icelandic mostly to their siblings and not exclusively so. Most participants in the survey were able to read and write Icelandic as children. Those surveyed who always spoke Icelandic as youngsters ranged in age from forty-five to eighty-six at the time they were surveyed in 1986. Only three speakers were under sixty-five (Birna Arnbjörnsdóttir, unpublished surveys).

VARIATION IN NORTH AMERICAN ICELANDIC

Two types of change characterize development of NA Icelandic. First, there have been changes due to language contact in the form of direct borrowings from English, both overt borrowings and substratum influences in t he lexicon and grammar. Second, there have been changes in the form of levelling and simplification caused by language attrition and the fact that NA Icelandic has narrowed greatly in its functional range.

Haraldur Bessason (1984b) defines NA Icelandic as a separate, geographically defined dialect of Icelandic. This is b orne out by the results of this study. However, this should not be construed to mean that NA Icelandic is one regular, consistent, and homogenous language variety. I expected to find a gradual formation of a more homogeneous dialect from one generation to another, similar to what Omdal found in his st udy of three generations of inhabitants and newcomers in Höyanger, Norway (1976, 1977, in T rudgill 1983, Ch. 3). It would probably be more accurate to characterize NA Icelandic as consisting of several regional subvarieties, familylects, and idiolects. That is, different settlements may have developed separate dialectal features as suggested by many of the informants, but so did families and even individuals. Subvarieties are thus made up of familylects and idiolects, both in the traditional sense as having the general idiosyncratic characteristics of individual speakers, and also reflecting the different ranges of embeddedness of English influences into the grammar of Icelandic that vary vastly from speaker to speaker (Vilhjálmur Stefánsson 1903; H araldur Bessason 1967, 1984a; Birna Arnbjörnsdóttir 1989, 1990c).

North American Icelandic is at various stages of attrition, regionally and individually, which contributes to the heterogeneity of the variety. Vilhjálmur Stefánsson reported on this variation as early as in 1903. N orth American Icelandic is a separate dialect in the sense that there seem to be certain grammatical and lexical features consistently found in the speech of a cross-section of its speakers.

As more speakers become English-dominant, more English transfer appears that can no longer be considered code switching but rather is lexical and grammatical transfer at various levels of embeddedness in Icelandic. An extreme example is the total integration of Icelandic names into English morphology and phonology. Other examples of transfer are the overwhelming use of English functions of Icelandic prepositions, and the categorical shift of impersonal verbs to personal verbs to comply with the usage of their English cognates. Internal language changes begin to appear in the form of convergence of linguistic features, simplification of rules, etc. Finally, there are general signs of language attrition of marked features in Icelandic, such as loss of umlaut, unrounding of front rounded vowels, loss of the voiced velar fricative, confusion in use of subjunctive, etc. (Birna Arnbjörnsdóttir 1990c, 1992a; Hill 1993).

A prominent change in the phonology are the mergers of long /I/ and /E/, so that words such as *við* 'us' and *vEð* 'collateral' become homonyms. This feature was brought to North America in the speech of the first generation of immigrants. There was clear evidence of increased spread of this feature from the oldest to the youngest generation of the informants. Informants from North Dakota had a higher frequency of vowel mergers (Flámæli) in their speech than informants from New Iceland. This is to be expected, as New Icelanders were more insulated from the outside world than their cousins in North Dakota where Icelanders were more integrated with other ethnic groups in the region.

The literature on language attrition seems to indicate that na Icelandic may indeed have a longer lifespan than many other immigrant languages. It is especially interesting that, although influenced by its proximity with English, NA Icelandic remains a basically intact language with respect to many of the simplification processes that have been reported for such other immigrant languages in the US and Canada as Finnish, Pennsylvania Dutch (a variety of German—Dutch is an Anglicized version of Deutsch or German), and Gaelic. Among Finns in America, by the second generation, only the eldest child in the family had more than a passive knowledge of Finnish, and those who knew Finnish showed limited sentence structure. Also, the inflectional system was found to be breaking down as well as the rules of vowel harmony. First-generation Finns showed massive lexical loss in their Finnish (Kartunnen 1977, p. 175). Haugen (1956) mentioned that Norwegians' adoption of English might have been accelerated by the dialectal differences found in Norwegian, hampering communication in the native language.

In a study of the Pennsylvania Dutch of the old order Mennonites in Ontario and Pennsylvania, Anderson and Martin (1976; in Lambert and Freed 1982) found attrition in the loss of umlaut and a loss of the bilabial fricative. In the morphology, they found loss of genitive case, collapse of accusative and nominative, and loss of dative case.

The linguistic and cultural attitudes of the NA Icelanders might prove to be more similar to that of the socially isolated Mennonites and the Amish than the situation of the other Scandinavian immigrant groups, although the loss of morphological rule is not as severe in NA Icelandic as in Pennsylvania Dutch. It is possible that the changes in Pennsylvania Dutch may be tied to the differences in length of stay in America. The German Mennonites began arriving about 100 years before the Icelanders; on the other hand, German immigration continued after the Icelandic immigration stopped, allowing for reinforcement of the language in some communities.

Nancy Dorian introduced the concept of "semi-speaker" in her study of Gaelic (1981, p. 114). These are speakers who are not quite proficient in the language; they speak a simplified version, having lost some of the more complex rules. Dorian found departures from the language norm in the case system and in the use of passives that went unnoticed by the community. She also found gender confusion and variable use of rules that, before, were not optional in earlier forms of Gaelic. The concept "semi-speaker" is not appropriate to use for any of the informants in this study, as there is no evidence of complete rule loss, either at the speech community level or at the individual level.

Unlike the many attrition histories of the languages reported in the literature (Dorian, Dressler, and others), this particular language variety will apparently not go through a stage of severe simplification and "semi-speakers," but will die out as the speakers pass away.

Several generalizations can be made about the process of language creation and attrition. It is a rare opportunity to gain insight into language change and language death as it happens not only of this particular variety but also of language in general. Many of the same factors that seem to have fostered linguistic conservatism in Iceland have also affected North American Icelandic. There are only minor simplifications found in the morphology, phonology, and syntax. Some of the changes taking place in NA Icelandic occur in areas where there seems to be a "drift" or unrest in modern Icelandic. This is Sapir's (1921) "native drift." This "drift" is especially noticeable in the morphology, specifically in the assignment of case by impersonal verbs, and by vowel mergers in the phonology, both present in modern Icelandic.

CONCLUSION

Why is it that some immigrant languages survive longer than others and some minority cultures thrive alongside the host culture, while others disappear or seem in conflict? Why is it that some immigrant groups are able to make the transition more successfully to a new way of life than others? The general assumption has been that bilingualism leads to social and educational failures. Bilingual educational models are, more often than not, deficit models. The current debate on bilingualism and bilingual education is broadened by the inclusion of a discussion of factors that are likely to lead to a successful transition into a second culture. There is much to be learned about the positive aspects of bilingualism and biculturalism from the linguistic and cultural history of the Icelandic immigrants in North American Icelanders. Their history suggests that pride in one's heritage, a commitment to access to literacy and education, and a comfort with, and acceptance of, bilingualism and biculturalism can lead to the development of sustained, intergenerational bilingualism and a successful transition to a new culture that is informed by the past and accepting of the future.

CHAPTER 3 **THE NORTH AMERICAN ICELANDIC LEXICON**

THE SOURCES

I have compiled the data for this section from several sources. Most of the lexical items come from Haraldur Bessason's (1967) important article on borrowings in NA Icelandic, based on interviews he conducted in the early 1960s prior to the extensive communications and contact that ensued between NA Icelanders and Iceland in the 1970s. Other sources are unpublished interviews collected in New Iceland, Manitoba, by Hallfreður Örn Eiríksson (1974) and by Gísli Sigurðsson (1982). Information also comes from Icelandic newspapers printed in Manitoba. Some of the loanwords come from my own interviews with NA Icelanders from the fall of 1986. That speech sample included thirty-eight informants from thirty to eighty-three years old. Seventeen informants lived in or around Mountain, North Dakota, and twenty-one informants lived in New Iceland in Manitoba. The raw data gathered for that study are available at the University of Iceland's Linguistic Institute.

All in all, the database for the general description in this chapter includes over 100 hours of interviews with approximately 100 informants. As sampling methods varied from study to study, some of the variation found in the data might be due to informants' using different registers and/or adjusting their speech because they were being interviewed.

DEGREES OF ASSIMILATION AND LEVELLING

There are several degrees of assimilation of English borrowings into Icelandic. They range from partial assimilation, as the words "township" and "range," to complete integration of the borrowings into productive rules of Icelandic (syntactic, semantic, phonological, and phonetic), such as in *baslari* 'bachelor' and *loggahús* 'log cabin'.

Vilhjálmur Stefánsson (1903) points out that there is "no uniformity of pronunciation" among loanwords in the speech of Icelandic immigrants living in North Dakota (p. 355). He also mentions the variation in the degree of "mixing" among individuals in the settlement (p. 355). Some speakers might borrow heavily from English while many "use scarcely one of the words" in his list. It is, therefore, difficult to determine the degree of integration of the words on his list into NA Icelandic. It is not clear whether any of the words on his list come from spontaneous code switching, but the same variation in assimilation of loanwords in the speech of different individuals seems to be true today.

The degree of assimilation of loanwords by individual speakers also varies, where some people use the English version of a word while others pronounce the same word according to Icelandic morphological, phonological, and phonetic rules. There is one exception to this. North American Icelandic proper nouns such as family names and place names have become Anglicized and are not declined according to Icelandic morphology rules. Names retain their English characteristics in otherwise Icelandic speech parts. This is the case for the twenty-five or so Icelandic place names approved for Manitoba by the Canadian Board of Place Names (Haraldur Bessason 1967, p. 137). Names like Arborg, Baldur, Bifrost, Gimli, Mikley, Hecla Island, and Lundar are found on Manitoba maps and pronounced according to English phonetic rules. Arborg is pronounced [arbərg] instead of the Icelandic [auRboRk]. The woman's name Erla /ER̥la/ with unvoiced /R̥/ and /l̥/ in Icelandic is pronounced /ərla/ in English. This custom is carried over to references to place names in Iceland that are generally not declined but always appear in nominative.

To this day the tradition of using patronymics with the ending *son* 'son' for men and *dóttir* 'daughter' for women is retained in Iceland. Haraldur Bessason discussed the adaptation of Icelandic names and naming customs into English in his 1967 article. His informants described some of the practical reasons why their forefathers felt compelled to change their names:

> My father Björn Guðmundsson Núpdal, adopted the family name Núpdal after he came to America, because his mail would often be sent to the home of a namesake who shared the services of the same post office.
>
> Jón Björnsson adopted the surname Snæfeld because another Jón Björnsson used the same post office as he.
>
> My grandfather, Pétur Jónsson, settled in a district in Saskatchewan among so many Jónssons that he was compelled to adopt the surname Norman. When doing so, he had in mind his native district in northern Iceland. (1967, p. 134 [translation Haraldur Bessason])

Surely, lost mail notwithstanding, the Icelandic immigrants, especially those living in Winnipeg, must have been under pressure to change their names and conform to the naming customs of their adopted country. It is not convenient to go around with a name no one can pronounce and loyalties to the name may have diminished when it no longer sounded like one's own name when pronounced by the locals. It is embarrassing in the new culture for children not to have the same name as their parents, for wives not to have the same name as their husbands and so on. I recognize, from first-hand experience, the problems faced living in an English speaking country with a last name like Arnbjörnsdóttir. Explaining the patronymic Icelandic naming system and why the different members of the family have different names soon becomes tiresome. So it must have been for the Icelanders who immigrated to North America. Keeping the old patronymic customs outside the Icelandic community may also have seemed unsophisticated and pointless, so they were soon abandoned and a family name tradition adopted. It is a well-known characteristic, especially of second-generation immigrants, to make specific efforts to conform to the new culture. Theirs is the first generation whose loyalties are divided between the heritage culture of their parents and the culture of the new country.

Adoption of family names was not random. Haraldur Bessason divides them into two main groups, both based on traditions already found in Iceland: one group contains names derived from the possessor's place of origin; the other involves Anglicizing the Icelandic last name. Both were common practices among the newly formed Icelandic bourgeoisie in the nineteenth century who made their names sound Danish and adopted them as family names.

These are some examples of the first group of adopted family names from Haraldur Bessason's sources: Axford (Axarfjörður), Bardal (Bárðardalur), Eyford (Eyjafjörður), Fljozdal (Fljótsdalur), Hofteig (Hofteigur), Hornfjord (Hornafjörður), Lundal (Lundareykjadalur), Midford (Miðfjörður), Oddstead (Oddstaðir), Ruth (Hrútafjörður), Skafel (Skaftafell or Skaftafellssýsla), Skardal (Gönguskörð), Strong (Strönd), Thistilford (Þistilfjörður), Vopni and Wopnford (Vopnafjörður).

Anglicizing the Icelandic patronyms was the other source of North American Icelandic family names. Needless to say, women who, upon marriage in Iceland, would have kept their maiden names, being identified as their fathers' daughters as in Jónsdóttir (daughter of Jón) or Árnadóttir (daughter of Árni), now took on their husbands' names and became son of Jón or son of Árni, as did their daughters. Here are some examples of Anglicized names: Anderson (Andrésson or Árnason), Benson (Benediktsson or Benjamínsson or Björnsson), Bearnson (Bjarnason), Byron (Björnsson), Gillies or Gillis (Gíslason), Goodman, Goodmon, or Goodmanson (Guðmundsson), Henderson (Helgason), Howard (Hávarðsson), Johnson or Johnston (Jónsson, Jóakimsson, and Jóhannesson), Martin (Marteinsson), Oleson (Eyjólfsson), Olsson (Ólafsson), Simpson or Siverz (Sigurðsson), Stephanson or Stephenson (Stefánsson), Summers (Sumarliðason), Swinburne (Sveinbjörnsson), Tait (Teitsson), Thompson (Tómasson), Thornsson (Þórarinsson), Thorson (Þórðarson), Walters, Walterson (Sigvaldason). To this list could be added Goodmans, Paulson, Peterson, Samson, and Jackson, and a host of names that were retained but acquired English pronunciation such as Bjornson, Finnbogason, Gislason, Kristinson, and Thomasson, etc. A family of informants in this study had changed the orthography of their family name so that its pronunciation would be closer to the original. Thus Sæmundsson became Simundsson.

In a few cases, Haraldur Bessason's informants' names were translations of an Icelandic topographical name, such as Hillman for Icelandic *bakki* 'bank, elevation' (Haraldur Bessason 1967, p. 134).

In some instances given names were also Anglicized, as in Bert for Dagbjartur or Henry for Hinrik, Ellen for Elín. Terms of endearment or abbreviated versions of Icelandic names, previously only limited to most familiar situations, became given names in North America. Clearly there were pragmatic reasons for this as the names were often difficult for the locals to pronounce. Such is the case for Siggi for Sigurður or Mundi for Guðmundur (Haraldur Bessason 1967, p. 135).

Naming traditions in the Icelandic communities follow trends seen among other immigrants. The 1920–21 church records from the First Icelandic Lutheran Church in Winnipeg show that 31% of children baptized received purely Icelandic names, 22% were given Icelandic and English names, and 47% received English names. In 1950 only 3% received Icelandic names and 82% received English names. In the Icelandic settlement of Arborg in 1920, Icelandic names were given to 57% of the children. In 1950, the majority of children received English names and no child received a purely Icelandic name, and only a third received Icelandic and English names (Haraldur Bessason 1967, pp. 136–37). Today, naming with Icelandic names the children who are the fourth and fifth generation from the original Icelandic settlers is quite popular—an indication of assimilation's having come full circle as curiosity about one's heritage increases among assimilated Canadians and Americans of Icelandic ancestry.

There was not a great deal of code-switching in general in the interviews I conducted, and some informants apologized when they reverted to using loanwords. Many of the informants spoke of the "mixing" of the two languages and some confessed that they did more mixing among themselves than they did in the interviews. This is a clear example of the difficulty in collecting truly representative speech. However, it may be an indication of the variety found in NA Icelandic in that many loanwords are not in the repertoire of all speakers, and of the degree to which they are incorporated into the phonology, morphology, and syntax of the language varies, as well.

THE LEXICON

The lexicon of North American Icelandic reflects a changing culture, a changing way of life in the new world demographically and diachronically. North American Icelandic has numerous lexical additions—both borrowings and neologisms mostly in semantic fields related to geography, technology, education, farming, and fishing as the settlers shifted from a coastal culture to an inland culture, from mixed farming and fishing to agriculture and lake fishing, from home schooling to formal education. Needless to say, almost all the loanwords come from English, although Haraldur Bessason (1967) reports that there may be terms borrowed from Ukrainian and the indigenous Athabascan languages as well. None of these were found in this data. It is interesting that many of the words presented have found their way directly into modern Icelandic from English, requiring a reanalysis of the data from the submission of the original thesis in 1990. Phrases like *Hvurnig er ég að gera?* 'How am I doing?' were unheard of in 1986 in Iceland, but in 2006 the overuse of present + infinitive seems to be a characteristic of speech of young Icelanders.

As expected, most of the lexical borrowings in NA Icelandic come from the open morphological classes—nouns, verbs, and adjectives (see Haugen 1950)—but there are several interesting changes in closed morphological classes (pronouns, conjunctions, and prepositions). According to Haraldur Bessason (1967), "among loan words in AI, nouns are by far the most common and constitute a much larger group than the verbs that form the second largest category" (p. 132). Adjectives and adverbs are also found but in much fewer numbers. Studies of other high language-contact situations attest to cross-linguistic borrowing taking place within closed morphological classes (Hudson 1980). In North American Icelandic, there seems to be a general transfer of English conjunctions or connector words in otherwise totally Icelandic sentences. Prepositions in NA Icelandic reflect a semantic shift as the Icelandic form of the preposition is used but the function of its

English cognate governs its usage. Subsequently, the cases that these prepositions assign have changed (see, for example, *fyrir* 'for' in Chapter 5). The use of the pronoun *þú* 'you' has been extended to include use as an indefinite pronoun. This is found in all the sources I examined but this interesting and telling example comes from Haraldur Bessason: 'Ef þú hefir verið hér lengi, og þér líkar vel í þessu landi, þá fer það oftast svo, að þú flytur ekki heim aftur' (If you have been here long, and if you like it in this country, then the upshot is in most cases that you do not go back home again) (1967, p. 131 [translation by Haraldur Bessason]).

The greatest changes in the grammar seem to be a result of substratum influences from English perhaps borrowed into earlier forms of NA Icelandic and acquired by later generations of speakers as their native grammar. The two languages share many etymologically related words. In some cases, apparent language attrition characteristics in the morphology are, upon closer inspection, due to semantic shift of a cognate where the Icelandic form is retained but the English function governs its usage. This is the case for the verb *vanta* 'want', which in Icelandic has a narrower meaning than 'want', but has taken on the meaning of 'want' in NA Icelandic and covers verbs like *vilja* and is/has been learned as such by younger speakers.

In this description only those English words and phrases are included that seem to have been reclassified as Icelandic; i.e., words that have been incorporated to different degrees into the structure of NA Icelandic and that appear with some frequency in the speech of more than one informant. This classification seems to comply with traditional definitions of borrowings (Weinreich 1953; Haugen 1950; Hudson 1980; Bynon 1977; Scotton 1988). Words, phrases, and sentences are seen as being code switched when they are "spontaneous insertions of an embedded language into a matrix language" (Scotton 1988, p. 318). The distinction between code switching and borrowing is not made in previous studies of the NA Icelandic lexicon, so it is difficult to say which words from those studies exemplify which phenomena.

There is reason to believe that in the last decades NA Icelandic has moved somewhat closer to standard Icelandic. Since 1975 visits by Icelanders to the immigrant communities as well as visits to Iceland by North American Icelanders have become commonplace and communications with Iceland have increased. Many of the informants had been to Iceland and corresponded with relatives or friends there. The amount of contact with Iceland or Icelanders varied from one informant to another but it seems that this may have affected the use of English borrowings in NA Icelandic. For example, two informants used the modern Icelandic colloquial form *rúta* instead of the more common NA Icelandic *böss* for 'bus', and one person used the modern Icelandic form *bíll* instead of the more common *kar* 'car'. When asked, all three acknowledged the more frequent use of *böss* and *kar*. It is interesting to note that neither of these words is on the list compiled by Vilhjálmur Stefánsson in 1903. But he does include the word 'automobile' and its gender varied from masculine to feminine and even neuter (p. 357). One informant who had never been to Iceland used the modern Icelandic slang expression *alveg magnað* 'powerful, amazing'. Another person informed us that his Icelandic had 'improved' greatly after having employed an Icelandic farmhand for a year.

ASSIGNMENT OF GENDER AND DECLENSION CLASSES

A discussion of loanwords in Icelandic is incomplete without mention of what grammatical gender was assigned to borrowed nouns and how they were declined. Vilhjálmur Stefánsson states that there seemed to be consistency in gender assignment of English nouns among the Icelandic immigrants. Of the 467 loanwords on his list, 176 were assigned neuter gender, 137 received masculine gender, and only 44 received feminine gender. There was some inconsistency regarding assignment of neuter or feminine (fifty-five words) or neuter or masculine (thirty), or all three (twenty), but only four words were either masculine or feminine in his data. Haraldur Bessason presents a list of 360 loanwords, 47% of which have neuter gender, 29% have masculine gender, and 20% are feminine. Only 4% show variation in gender. This list is compiled some sixty-four years after Vilhjálmur´s taxonomy of loanwords and it suggests that their use has stabilized.

The motivation for assigning grammatical gender may have been, in some cases, the ending of the word (Vilhjálmur Stefánsson 1903; Haraldur Bessason 1967). For example, words that ended in –or, –er, or –r received masculine gender and were declined according to the strong masculine category that includes *hestur* and *hamar* with nominative plural –ar. These include words like *skollar* 'scholar', *klíner* 'cleaner', *djindjer* 'ginger', *ventileitor* 'ventilator', and *stír* 'steer'. But there are exceptions to this, like *ringer*, which is neuter. According to Vilhjálmur Stefánsson, words ending in –l or –ll generally became neuter as in *beisbol* 'base-ball', but there is a counter example *fútbol* 'foot-ball' that is masculine. Examining the grammatical gender of the loan nouns in the data was beyond the scope of this study. Very little is known about how second-language learners learn grammatical gender and closer inspection of how loanwords received gender in NA Icelandic could provide important insight into the universal characteristics of how and why adults seem to be consistent in assigning the same words to the same grammatical categories.

LOANWORDS

From the outset of Icelandic settlement in North America, English has been incorporated into NA Icelandic. In the first code of laws of New Iceland, printed in the newspaper *Framfari* in 1878, English loanwords are found within Icelandic sentences:

> Landnám Íslendinga í Nýja-Íslandi nefnist Vatnsþing; það skal skiptast í fjögur byggðalög, er nefnist Víðinesbyggð, er innibindi townshipin No. 18 og 19, Range 3 og 4 austur (East).
>
> /The Icelandic settlement in New Iceland is named Vatnsþing; it is divided into four settlements named Víðinesbyggð which incorporates township no. 18 and 19, Range 3 and 4 East/. (in Haraldur Bessason 1967, p. 115)

The loanwords 'township' and 'range' are still used in NA Icelandic today and there is no evidence to show that attempts have been made to translate them. *Innibindi* is another interesting word, probably archaic and found in older varieties of Icelandic. Notice however, that *townshipin* has the Icelandic neutral, plural, nominative ending, which is common practice with loanwords and in code switching—i.e., Icelandic morphological endings are attached to English loanwords. Vilhjálmur Stefánsson (1903) gives a list of some 462 English loanwords used by Icelandic speakers in his native North

Dakota settlement. Since Vilhjálmur Stefánsson's list is a cen tury old and compiled some twenty-five years after the first Icelanders came to North Dakota, it is difficult to determine the lifespan of many of the words on the list. Some archaic forms, like *lap-robe, knotter*, and *graphophone*, have fallen out of use in standard spoken English and for the same reason have fallen out of use in NA Icelandic.

Another list o f characteristic borrowings is p resented in H araldur Bessason (1967). This list is probably more representative in that by the time he conducted his study, NA Icelandic had been isolated for almost ninety years with very few contacts with standard Icelandic after the first forty years or so. A representative list of lexical borrowings expanded from Haraldur Bessason (1967) is presented below with some added words from my study and from a short list f ound on the Icelandic-Canadian Web site from 2003 <h ttp://www.umanitoba.ca/faculties/arts/icelandic/IceCan/language.htm>.

Pure Loanwords and Additions

This category contains words that are borrowed without much change from one language to another except in p ronunciation. It is deba table whether some of these words should not go into the loan blend category. Notice that some of the words have also been borrowed into modern Icelandic from English.

A note about the broad transcription below: there are no voiced stops /b, d, g/ in I celandic pronunciation even though they are found in the orthography. As this is carried over into pronunciation of foreign languages, below-voiced stops in En glish loanwords in Icelandic are represented as v oiceless stops /p, t, k/. Aspirated voiceless stops are represented as /ph, th, kh/. Notice also that double consonants can sometimes be preaspirated. This is indicated by /hk/ or /ht/.

NA Icelandic	Icelandic	English
Nouns:		
*address (fem.)	/atREs:/	address
*akkordion (nt.)	/akɔRtion/	accordion
ambjúlans (masc.)	/ampyulans/	ambulance

beisment (nt.)	/pesmEnt/	basement
bojfrend (nt.)	/bɔyfREnt/	boyfriend
bröss (masc.)	/pRös:/	bush/brush
böss (masc.)	/pös:/	bus
dokk (fem.)	/tɔhkh/	dock
greid (nt. fem.)	/kre:t/	grade
fón (masc.)	/fon/	phone
kanú (masc.)	/kha:nu/	canoe
kar (nt.)	/kha:R/	car
kart (nt.)	/khaRth/	cart
kjeik (fem.)	/khyekh/	cake
keikur, keikar, keiks (plural)	/khyekhs/	cakes
kort (nt.)	/khɔRt/	court
kót (nt.)	/khot/	coat
loggur (masc.)	/lɔk:YR/	log
loggi (masc.)	/lɔk:yI/	log
lód (nt.)	/lot/	load
mús (nt.)	/mu:s/	moose
nörs/nörsa (fem.)	/nöRs/	nurse
póni (masc.)	/phonI/	pony
reins (nt.)	/Rens/	range
stasjón (fem.)	/stašyon/	station
sjanti (masc.)	/šanthI/	shanty
*sjó (nt.)	/šo/	show
skar (nt.)	/skaR/	scar
skonkur (masc.)	/skɔnkYR/	skunk
stír (masc.)	/stiR/	steer
*söksess (?)	/sök:sEs:/	success
tím (nt.)	/ti:m/	team
tánsjip (nt.)	/thaunšIph/	township
trökk (fem.)	/thRökh/	truck
trakkir (fem. pl.)	/tRahky:IR]	trucks
trögg (fem.)	/thRök/	truck
tæjer (nt.)	/thaiyER/	tire
veiter (masc.)	/vetER/	waiter
vúllur (masc.)	/vul:YR/	wool

önderteiker (masc.) /öntERthekER/ undertaker
* Also found in modern Icelandic

Verbs:
boðra /pɔðRa/ bother
borða /pɔRða'/ board
fóna /foːna/ phone
fylla inn /tIhl̥a/ fill in
settla /sEhtla/ settle
fitta inn /fIhtha Inː/ fit in
klína /klina/ clean
*meina /mena/ mean
*mixa /mIksa/ mix
rósta /Rosta/ roast

Adjectives:
bisí /pIsi/ busy
næs /nais/ nice
sjúr /šyuR/ sure
smart /smaRth/ smart

*Also found in modern Icelandic.

Loan Blends

Loan blends seem to be made of part English and part Icelandic words. Most often, the root morpheme is borrowed from English, whereas the derivational morpheme or ending comes from Icelandic, allowing the word to fit into Icelandic morphological paradigms. Here are some examples:

Nouns:
barði (fem.) /paRðI/ barge
blakkborð /plahkbɔRð/ blackboard
brússki /pRuskI/ bush/brush
busski /puskI/ bush
dröggbúð /tRökːbuð/ drugstore
farmari (masc.) /faRmaRI/ farmer
hestakar /hEstakhaR/ horse carriage
húddtreyja /hutːthRea/ hood jacket

jólakarð	/yolakhaRð/	Christmas card
kattfiskur	/khathfIskYR/	catfish
loggahús	/lɔk:ahus/	log house
loggakofi	/lɔk:akɔvI/	log cabin
lombermylla	/lɔmpERmIl:a/	lumber mill
kontrískóli	/khɔnthRiskolI/	country school
korðviður	/khɔRðvIðYR/	wood
korðviðarspýta	/kɔRðvIðaRsphita/	wooden stick
músdýr	/mus:tiR/	moose
rabbítur.(masc.)	/Rap:itYR/	rabbit
rakki	/Rak:I/	rack
spilakarð	/spIlakhaRð/	playing card
sprústré	/spRusthryE/	spruce tree
steibla (fem.)	/stepla/	stable
stikka	/stIk:a/	stick
tóstari (masc.)	/thostaRI/	toaster
tæjur (nt.)	/thaiyYR/	tire

Loanwords that Cause Semantic Reinterpretation, Semantic Narrowing, or Semantic Extension

Icelandic and English share many words that have similar, or the same, etymologies. Often, in t hose cases where the words occur with some frequency, the Icelandic form is used but the English function is preferred. Notice the number of verbs in this category.

NA Icelandic	English	Stand. Icelandic Meaning
Nouns:		
baslari	bachelor	struggler
bóur	bow	bow
bryggja/briggja	bridge	dock
Enskir	N Americans other than Icelanders	the English
gólf	1ˢᵗ, 2ⁿᵈ floor	floor
háskóli	high school	university
ʔhúð	animal hide	skin

nón	noon	3 o'clock
pláss	place	space
punktur	point (geograph.)	period
rafmagnsstrætiskör	electric streetcars	
skar	scare	old frail person
stó	stove	fireplace
strætiskar	streetcar	
stykki	piece of land	piece
tími	time	period
þorpari	townsperson	rogue

Verbs:

basla	to be a bachelor	struggle
búa	make	live/farm
draga	draw	pull
fara gegnum	go through experience	lit. meaning
hafa	have	possess
hugsa	believe, think	believe
kalla	call/phone	shout
*meina	mean	mean
mæta	meet	pass by
lifa	live/reside	to be alive
líka	like	like (narrower)
vanta	want	need
vinna	gain/win	work/win
sýnast	it looks like	it seems to s-e

*Found in modern Icelandic.

Adjectives:

hart	hard	much
mest af	most of	the majority of
stuttur	short of money	physically short
þunnur	slim	thin/hung over

Prepositions:

fyrir	for	for

Loan Translations (Calques)

A *calque* is a loanword whose form and meaning are indirectly transferred into another language. "Instead of being carried over into the recipient language as a unit, [it] is merely employed as a model for a native creation" (Bynon 1977, p. 232).

NA Icelandic	English	Icelandic
Nouns:		
borðhús	boarding house	gistihús
blæjur	blinds	gardínur?
brauðláf	loaf of bread	brauð, brauðhleifur
gesthús	guest house	gististaður
hreyfimynd	motion picture	kvikmynd
hreyfimyndasýning	motion picture show	kvikmyndasýning
ísrjómi	ice cream	rjómaís
ljóshús	lighthouse	viti
maskína	machine	vél
yfirskór	overshoes	bomsur?
eftirnón	afternoon	síðdegis
*tengdabróðir	brother-in-law	mágur
*tengdasystir	sister-in-law	mágkona

*The Icelandic word for mother-in-law is *tengdamóðir*, and father-in-law is *tengdafaðir*, whereas brother-in-law and sister-in-law are *mágur* and *mágkona*, respectively. In NA Icelandic, mágur and mágkona have been changed by analogy to *tengdabróðir* and *tengdasystir*.

Verbs:		
vatna blóm	water flowers	vökva (blóm)

Archaisms

The following list includes words that may have been common in the Icelandic the settlers brought with them but are uncommon or no longer found in modern standard Icelandic. Many are words borrowed from Danish and were later considered to be markers of inferior Icelandic in Iceland and dropped. (For an illuminating discussion about this, especially the demise of the verb *ske* in Icelandic, see Veturliði Óskarsson 1997–1998.)

Nouns:

búningur	costume	used in mod. Icelandic almost exclusively for theatrical costumes but had a more general meaning in older forms
bytta	small boat	archaic
etasjur	floors	Danish, rare
família	family	Danish, rare
haldabrauð	bread	rare in mod. Icelandic
krít	crayon	Danish, rare
langi (masc.)	sausage	rare in mod. Icelandic
langa (fem.)	sausage	"
loðtreyja	fur jacket	"
nafar	drill	"
polití	police	"
treyja	sweater	archaic form
totta	pacifier	archaic form
Franskanj	French (noun)	archaic

Verbs:

brúka	use	an older Danish loanword not common in modern Icel. but found in older forms
skeinkja	pour (coffee)	Danishism

Adjectives:

býsna	very	?archaic

Adverbs:

billegt	cheap	Danishism
allareiðu	already	Danishism

Neologisms

North American Icelanders often created new Icelandic words for things for which they had no word.

NA Icelandic	English	Modern Icelandic
Nouns:		
braut	highway	þjóðvegur/þjóðbraut
draghnífur	drawknife/dragknife	?
flugskip	airplane	flugvél/flugbátur?
gufuketill	steam engine	eimreið
hestafjós	stable	hesthús
ketill	engine	eimreið
kindafjós	sheepshed	kindakofi
krossbraut	crossroads	krossgötur
kúafjós	cowshed	fjós
kyndibox	cinderbox?/matches	eldspýtnakassi?
loftbátur	airplane	flugvél
mál/málolía	paint	málning
svínafjós	pigsty	svínastía

Multi-word Borrowings/Conventions

Very few of the numerous sayings and expressions that characterize Icelandic speech are present in NA Icelandic. However, several English phrases and speech conventions have made their way into Icelandic, translated, and used with some frequency. Most of these would make little sense to a non-English-speaking Icelander. Some of the borrowed conventions include the omission of *hundruð* 'hundred' in dates; e.g., *átján sjötíu og sex* 'eighteen seventy-six' instead of the traditional *átján hundruð sjötíu og sex* 'eighteen hundred and seventy six'. Also, the uses of the past tense in reference to date or place of birth; e.g., *ég var fædd* 'I was born', instead of the traditional Icelandic *ég er fædd* 'I am born'. Other English conventions of speech and translated idioms include:

í endanum á	at the end of
það var í endanum á maí.	It was at the end of May.

In Icelandic this phrase has a more literal meaning.

aftur á bak og áfram   to go to and fro
   In Icelandic this means literally to haul back and forth.

mest af tímanum   most of the time
Við tölum íslensku mest af tímanum   We speak English most of the time.
   This expression is not used in Icelandic.

frjósa up   freeze up
vatnið var fljótt að frjósa upp   The lake was quick to freeze up.
   This expression is not used in Icelandic.

hvurnig er ég að gera?   How am I doing?
   Interestingly, the overuse of the present continuous seems to be catching on in modern Icelandic also and is translated into the infinitive as in *að gera*. Fifteen years ago, this expression was considered ungrammatical in modern Icelandic. Now, even though it is not considered standard Icelandic, it is used, even in the most formal spoken registers.

Það er bytta til mín   It is a bytta to me.
   This expression is not used in Icelandic.

ofan við   on top of
mér var sagt að hann hafi slegið   I was told that he harvested for his
dag og dag fyrir nágranna sína ofan   neighbours on top of harvesting for
við það sem hann þurfti að heyja   himself.
í sína eigin gripi
   This expression is not used in Icelandic.

hluturinn er   the thing is
hluturinn er að það er búið að eyða...   The thing is that they have destroyed.
   This expression is not used in Icelandic.

renna út af   to run out of
   This expression is not used in Icelandic.

koma upp með   come up with
   This expression is not used in Icelandic.

að hafa band við Ísland   to have ties to Iceland
   This is another expression that fifteen years ago was considered non-Icelandic. Now the expression *að vera í bandi* is quite common especially among younger speakers, although the meaning is slightly different.

Oddities

Some borrowings defy categorization. Some of these are:

tresvoltis	some type of profanity
verslunarbúð	lit. a shopping shop
faðirfaðir	grandfather, from Danish *farfar*?
börnbörn	grandchildren, Icel. barnabörn

CONCLUSION

Lexicographers might find fault with some of the categorizations and interpretations above. Some words clearly could belong under more than one heading. Nor is this an exhaustive list of borrowings. It is an interesting topic for further study to examine what types of words were borrowed and how they were used. It would also be interesting to revisit the words and expressions found in NA Icelandic that have also found their way into modern Icelandic from English. Some of the data hails from the late sixties and early seventies and my own data was collected from the late eighties. At the time of this writing, a reanalysis was necessary for many of the words, as, over the course of thirty to forty years, they had become part of modern Icelandic. Again a word of warning: it is very difficult to determine which words are the results of code switching and which are legitimate members of the NA Icelandic lexicon. The words presented here were found in the speech repertoire of more than one speaker. The fact that more than one speaker uses the words could still merely be an indication that speakers are likely to transfer certain types of words and expressions from English to Icelandic. That, in and of itself, would be an interesting area of further study as it would shed light on the language use of bilinguals and when and how they switch from one language to another. It could also give some indication as to what types of lexical items are more likely to be transferred from one language to another.

CHAPTER 4 **COLLECTING THE DATA**

Milroy (1987) identifies two main issues that have implications for the field investigator in sociolinguistics: "the relationship of the investigator to data and the relationship between data and grammar" (p. 1). This chapter details the former of those issues; i.e., the methods and means by which the data for this study were collected. The method of analysis of Flámæli and the interpretation of its relationship to the grammar of Icelandic are the subjects of chapters 5 through 7. Methodologies and approaches available to those who study variation in language are discussed and efforts are made to place the methods used in this study within an appropriate theoretical framework. Then, the characteristics of the sampling communities are outlined: the means by which the informants were chosen; the characteristics of the informants; the methods used in eliciting the appropriate data; and the quantitative tools that were utilized for the analysis of the data.

CHOOSING THE RELEVANT THEORETICAL PARADIGM

Current methods of examining language variation synchronically have afforded us an opportunity to gain insight into diachronic evolution of language as it happens. This is the research orientation of this study; i.e., the view that by studying language at the level of its function—as a medium of expression among individuals whose language behaviour is governed by the norms and traditions laid down by the speech community to which they belong—we can gain insight into the nature and evolution of language, and understand better the factors that may have influenced language development in the past.

Walters (1988) identified four major "strands" of thought within sociolinguistics: the quantitative methods associated with urban dialectology (Labov, e.g. 1966, 1969, 1972a, 1972b; Trudgill 1972; Cedergren and Sankoff 1974; Baugh 1980); the investigation of role of the individual within a social network in the innovation and spread of change combined with quantitative methods as ex emplified by the work of the Milroys (1987) a nd others; Romaine's (1981) broader approach, which seeks to account for "Communicative Competence" as a whole; and Trudgill's "geolinguistics" or combination of dialect geography, urban dialectology, and human geography (Chambers and Trudgill 1980).

These approaches are not mutually exclusive; many linguists use a combination of two or more, depending upon the goals of their research. All approaches have the same ultimate goal, as outlined by Weinreich, Labov, and Herzog (1968): to account for the heterogeneity apparent in all sp eech communities, and eventually to shed light on how present linguistic patterns might explain diachronic linguistic change. Since the main objective of this study is to examine the nature and spread of a certain dialect feature, Flámæli, of North American Icelandic, Trudgill's geolinguistics provides the most effective framework. Variable rule analysis is used to quantify the effects of different social and linguistic factors on apparent vowel mergers in NA Icelandic, and the methods employed in collecting the appropriate data were guided by principles first put forth by Labov (1966, 1972a, 1972b, 1986) and by the network concept presented by Milroy and Milroy (1985). F inally, following Trudgill (1974) and others, the results of the quantitative analysis of synchronic variation (in apparent time) are used to re-examine the historical development of apparent mergers of four front vowels—(I), (Y), (E), and (ö)—in Icelandic (in real time). The data used for the general description of other features of NA Icelandic are a by-product of this study. Although variable rule analysis was only used to analyze the Flámæli features, Labovian collection methods provided representative data of the dialect overall.

THE SPEECH COMMUNITY

Collecting data that adequately represents the speech of the community under investigation requires three *a priori* decisions (Sankoff 1980). The first is to define the scope of the speech community. The second is to assess the possible stratification of that community, which may cause variability in the speech of the population. The third is to "fix the sample size" in terms of numbers of informants and amount of data (p. 51).

Data for this study was collected in two communities that are representative of the small number of rural Icelandic immigrant communities in North America. Neither community has "institutions" whose purpose it is to preserve Icelandic culture, but both are seen by the Icelandic immigrant community as the centres with the highest concentration of inhabitants of Icelandic descent in the United States and Canada.

New Iceland, Manitoba

New Iceland, which stretches north and south along the shores of Lake Winnipeg in Manitoba, is considered the bastion of Icelandic language and culture in North America. Although Winnipeg is the centre for "institutionalized" Icelandic culture in the new world, New Iceland is seen as its true "heart." It is mainly a farming community, but the towns of Gimli, Riverton, and Arborg were founded and inhabited by Icelanders and the region is "Icelandic" in its ethnicity, although other ethnic groups have moved in. Gimli has an annual Icelandic Festival, Íslendingadagurinn, in August, where such Icelandic traditions as the appearance of the *Fjallkona* ('Lady of the Mountain'), a symbol for Iceland, are part of the ceremonies. In recent years dignitaries and entertainers from Iceland have been part of the attractions at the festival. Businesses in many of the summer resorts on Lake Winnipeg carry Icelandic goods. A major resort on Hecla Island in Lake Winnipeg has an Icelandic name and theme, and Icelandic food on the menu. High schools in the area put on Icelandic plays (in English), and Icelandic is taught as a second language in Riverton. Icelandic Canadians, like other ethnic minorities in Canada, have benefited from Canada's supportive approach to preservation and retention of minority cultures.

Mountain, North Dakota

The settlements in and around Mountain in the most northeastern corner of North Dakota have been more isolated from Icelandic cultural activities than their counterparts in Manitoba. Although they look to Winnipeg as a cultural centre, national borders, distance, and probably the idea of the United States as a melting pot of nationalities have led to less emphasis on the preservation of Icelandic language and culture than across the border in Manitoba. Almost from the beginning of settlement, Mountain has had a minister from Iceland, but for the last few decades, religious services have been in English. Older members of the community meet on alternative weeks to socialize and play cards, but on two observational occasions, I heard almost no Icelandic except when I was s poken to directly. I obs erved two other social occasions in Mountain: the centennial anniversary of the first Icelandic church in North Dakota and an "Icelandic" picnic. Very little Icelandic was spoken on either of these occasions except in gr oups where one or more Icelandic guest was present.

Accessing the Speech Community

The representativeness of the data depends in part on appropriate sampling methods, including appropriate sampling of speakers. A variety of means by which a s ample community can be approached effectively has been used (Labov 1972b; Milroy and Milroy 1985; Bortoni-Ricardo and Maris 1985). In this study a "judgement sampling method" (Labov 1972a, 1972b; Ro maine 1981) was used as a means to engage the appropriate informants, for several reasons. The main reason was t hat random sampling, which in t he social sciences would offer a more "true representativeness," was impossible due to an absence of a dependable sample frame; i.e. a census or list available of all possible speakers of Icelandic in North America. Secondly, not all the inhabitants of either sample community are of Icelandic descent, and, of those who are, not all sp eak Icelandic. It was t hus necessary to find initial contact persons who were familiar enough with the sample community to be able to identify informants who met the specific criteria predetermined by the investigator, and who were compatible with the objectives of the study.

Initial contact in 1986 with the Icelandic immigrant communities was made through Haraldur Bessason, then of the University of Manitoba in Winnipeg. Professor Haraldur Bessason spent over twenty years in Winnipeg and was very much a leader in the "Icelandic" communities in Canada and North Dakota. He introduced me to an Icelandic-speaking farmer from the New Iceland region, as well as to the Icelandic minister of the Lutheran church in Mountain. Some problems arise in this type of sampling; one is the possibility that the contact person will select only those in his inner circle of friends and acquaintances. Or, as in the case where the contact person is a clergyman, that only churchgoing people will be represented. Efforts were made to minimize such a bias. The contact persons were carefully oriented as to the purpose of the study, and were instructed to select as informants only those who spoke Icelandic that was representative of the speech in the communities. They were also instructed to avoid people at either end of the continuum in terms of loyalty to their Icelandic heritage. Other informants, through suggestions and introductions, recruited additional informants. It must be kept in mind that the two speech communities have small populations. The inhabitants were acquainted with one another. The contact persons were able to select informants outside their innermost circle of friends. Efforts were made to have equal numbers of males and females in the sample, as well as equal numbers of people for each age group: 1) fifty and younger, 2) fifty to seventy, and 3) over seventy years old. It was not always possible to meet these criteria.

Characteristics of the Informants: Age and Sex

The decision about the appropriate size and characteristics of the informant sample is another issue that pertains to representativeness of the data. There seems to be no ideal size for the sample, except that it should not be too large (over 150 informants) (Sankoff 1980, p. 52). In this study the goal was to find an equal number of males and females from each locality, and equal numbers of informants for each of the three age groups. There were thirty-eight informants in the sample used for this study. Seven men and ten women were from Mountain, North Dakota. Eleven men and ten women were from New Iceland in Manitoba, for a total of eighteen men and twenty women across the two communities. Their ages ranged from thirty, the youngest, to eighty-three, the oldest. See Table 3 for distribution of informants according to locality, age, and sex.

TABLE 3

The Distribution of Informants by Locality, Age, and Sex

Location	- 50 Years	50–70 Years	70 + Years	# by Sex
New Iceland (F)	3	4	3	10
North Dakota (F)	2	4	4	10
New Iceland (M)	5	3	3	11
North Dakota (M)	2	2	3	7
Total by age	12	13	13	38

F = Female M = Male

Seven men and five women are in the youngest age category, five men and eight women in the middle category, and six men and seven women in the oldest category, or twelve informants in all in the youngest group, thirteen in the middle group, and thirteen in the oldest group. The grouping of informants according to age representing three generations was necessary in order to look at the spread of Flámæli through 'apparent time', as a 'real time' study could not be undertaken.

Three women in the middle age group were grouped as one. They were present at the same group interview but each of them, individually, did not contribute enough data to adequately represent individual speakers. Grouping informants in this manner is not ideal; however, it was deemed acceptable in this case as the women were of similar ages, were relatives, and lived together in one home.

Appropriateness of Traditional Social Stratification across Cultures

One of most important and most studied factors in the research of speech variation is that of social class. However, applicability of traditional social categories based on Western norms across cultures is an issue that linguists are beginning to question (Haeri 1989; Brown 1989; Walters 1988). Traditionally, such indicators as education, income, occupation, or quality of housing are used to determine an informant's social class or social status (Labov 1966, 1972a; Trudgill 1974). Applying these norms to the informants of this study was not possible. The majority of the informants live in rural farming communities where it seems that most people enjoy equal status. Most of my informants were very well read and informed about world events. Many of their children were university-educated professionals. These informants were "educated" farmers even though many of them did not enjoy a long formal education. No attempt was made, therefore, to categorize these informants in terms of their social or educational status; social status or social class was excluded as a factor in the use of Flámæli in this study.

Obtaining the Desired Speech Variety

The relationship between interviewer and interviewee and its effect on the quality of the data have been discussed by many linguists (Milroy 1987; Labov, throughout; G. Sankoff 1980; Shuy, Wolfram, and Riley 1968; Walters 1988). The status of "insider" or "friend of a friend" is often used to indicate better or closer ties to the community under investigation. The investigator thus gains access to better, more regular, colloquial speech. The definition of what constitutes an "insider" seems rather elusive in the literature and warrants further discussion.

Milroy (1987) discusses the advantage and disadvantage of having a linguistically trained "insider" do linguistic research in his/her own community. The advantage is that the "insider" is familiar with the norms and values of that particular community. The disadvantage is that the insider is often blinded by community-defined norms, which go unquestioned but which a more objective investigator, who is an outsider, is often able to see through.

In this study, the investigator was born and grew up in Iceland, thereby sharing some of the cultural background of the informants. Many of the traditions and behaviours observed in their homes were familiar to me. I recognized that these people were English-dominant bilingual and bicultural, who shared some of the home traditions one finds in Iceland. However, these people do not see themselves as being Icelandic and it would have been a mistake to assume that an Icelander would be considered an "insider" in the Icelandic immigrant communities in North America. One indicator of my status vis-à-vis the informants was the virtual lack of code switching in the interviews. Yet, several of the informants spoke about "mixing" the languages. "Mixing" English and Icelandic was the object of many puns and jokes among the informants. The informants obviously did not see me as "one of them," despite my having been introduced by a "friend," and thus made efforts to speak only Icelandic.

Taking this cue, and in an effort to maximize shared interests and maintain appropriate ethnosensitivity (Baugh 1980), I was always truthfully introduced to the informants as an expatriate Icelander who had lived and studied in the United States for a number of years. In accordance with Icelandic tradition, the conversations usually started with the informants or informant asking me about my origins in Iceland, whether there were relatives in the immigrant communities, and how the decision to study in Texas came about (the University of Texas is my alma mater). I made it a point to talk about the difficulties in keeping my two children bilingual, hoping to convey a sense that the informants did not need to defend how well they were preserving Icelandic culture in America. Establishing a common background was helpful. The informants shared the "human" side of the immigration story and the discussions were lively. Often, the presence of the tape recorder was totally forgotten.

The contact persons escorted me to most of the interviews, introduced me to the informants, and were present during some of the sessions, helping to establish a sense of my being considered a "friend of a friend." However, I was there as a linguist with a tape recorder, studying the speech patterns of these people, and this was known and accepted by all involved.

THE INTERVIEWS

Three basic axioms underlie a premise that has governed sociolinguistic studies for the last decades: there are no single-style speakers; attention to speech is least in the most informal speech styles; and the most informal speech style provides the most systematic linguistic data (Labov 1972b, pp.

208–209). Since there exists in a given speech community a somewhat consistent, informal vernacular, studying that speech variety gives the greatest insights into language at its most regular. It thus becomes the goal of sociolinguistic study to obtain data that best exemplifies this vernacular.

The interviews for this study were a combination of the individual interview (Shuy, Wolfram, and Riley 1968; Cedergren 1973; Trudgill 1972; and others) and group interviews (Blom and Gumperz 1986; Bortoni-Ricardo and Maris 1985; Milroy 1987), often with the investigator as a participant observer (Labov 1980). The interviews were taped on a Califone 3430 tape recorder, using a Sony FV30T table microphone.

Interviews lasted from about a half hour to several hours, depending on the number of participants (from individual to group interviews). In addition, the participants in the group discussions were interviewed individually (excluding the three women mentioned above, whose contributions were collapsed into one). The variables [I, E Y, ö] are quite frequent in the data (almost every word has one or more of the vowels in them). Thus, lengthy interviews were not deemed necessary for obtaining adequate amounts of data. The tape recorder ran from the moment I had been introduced and explained the purpose of the visit; i.e., during the setting up of the interview and introductory conversations, and through thank yous and farewells.

Three types of interview strategies were utilized. The first part of each interview was a general conversation, which lasted from twenty minutes up to several hours for group interviews. The topics of the conversations varied. Often personal histories were sought, although this was more difficult to do in group sessions. One topic that was always discussed was the experiences of the informants' ancestors when they came to the new world. This was an emotional subject for many of the informants, and had been chosen in an effort to elicit a register where the least amount of attention would be given to speech. This topic was seen as serving the same purpose as Labov's "close encounter with death" topic. Also, following Icelandic custom, current events naturally became the topic of many of the discussions.

Second, informants were asked, individually, to perform a picture identification task; in addition, they were encouraged to use the language and labels most natural to them. This task involved naming objects or actions illustrated in twenty-six pictures. In all cases, there was conversation during the performance of this task. Finally, some of the informants read short passages, which elicited Flámæli features specifically.

Using the three interview strategies was motivated by two goals. The first goal is to obtain data that exemplified three different speech styles: informal conversational style, reading style, and the most formal word list style. The second goal is to elicit specific dialectal information from the picture identification task and the reading task in order to facilitate eventual comparisons with results from a major dialect study of Iceland—i.e., RÍN (Rannsókn í íslensku nútímamáli)—underway in I celand at the time (H öskuldur Þráinsson and Kristján Árnason 1984, 1986; and others).

Attempts to elicit different speech styles from most informants proved fruitless. The data suggest that, given its narrowed functional range and the different levels of language attrition among its speakers, there may not be a regular, consistent vernacular form of North American Icelandic. Some of the informants obviously did not have different speech styles at their disposal, which deemed any comparison of speech across styles meaningless.

Group interviews have disadvantages and advantages. The disadvantages are that the quality of the recording may be poor, and it is difficult to make sure that equal amounts of data are elicited from all p resent. For example, in one interview, an older woman present did not say more than a few sentences. At another interview, the panting of the family dog s ometimes made the conversations of those present difficult to transcribe. In yet another session, the informant carried on lengthy conversations with her severely disabled adult son in a la nguage that only the mother and child could understand.

The advantages of group interviews, however, outweigh the disadvantages. Question-and-answer sessions, with the investigator controlling the topic, are avoided, and accommodation to the Icelandic speech of the investigator is minimized (M ilroy 1987, p. 41). The group sessions were more like actual conversations, albeit between hosts and guests who do not know each other very well. The group interviews were thus conversations often directed by an insider from the community or someone other than the investigator. Great care was taken to elicit casual, relaxed speech, and to maintain at all times eno ugh ethnosensitivity (Baugh 1980) s o as not to alienate the informants.

The individual interviews proved valuable in t hat specific features and background information could be elicited, which is difficult to do in a group.

Following Shuy, Wolfram, and Riley (1968), to claim that this data accurately represents "in-group" vernacular speech would be optimistic. It would be more accurate to suggest that the data is r epresentative of semiformal Icelandic speech between adults in the North American Icelandic immigrant communities—semiformal in t he sense that the informants were able to avoid code switching to a large extent.

ANALYZING VARIATION IN SPEECH

Variable rule analysis of synchronic variation was first developed by Labov (1966) in his st udy of linguistic variation in New York City. Labov (1966, 1972a) developed strict methods of measuring language change in progress, based on the presence of different social conditions and the occurrence and non-occurrence of grammatical features in a person's speech. He introduced a statistical analysis (Variable Rule Analysis) to account for the variation found in everyday speech, whereby a limited number of components representing linguistic and social contexts of a given rule could be used to predict each context's contribution to the probability of that rule's applying or not applying. The linguistic contexts could be the characteristics of the preceding or following sounds, the place in the words or syllables or even in a sentence, stress, and segment length, and social contexts could be sex, social class, age of the speaker, the topic, and setting of the conversation. To illustrate this with a well-known example: linguists now had the means to study the likelihood of, for example, when a speaker in New York City is likely to pronounce /r/ in his o r her speech, given the speaker's sex, education, social situation, and linguistic context (Labov 1966, 1972a).

Weinreich, Labov, and Herzog (1968) placed variation theory within a larger issue of language evolution. By comparing the behaviours of different age groups within the community, the direction of the linguistic change can be determined by the frequency of use by different generations. This is based on the assumption that if a feature change is indeed in p rogress, each generation will be more frequent users of that feature than the generation before, if the change is spreading. If the change is receding, then each generation will have the feature more frequently than the generation following. Trudgill (1972) further developed this methodology to plot the spread of a linguistic feature from one generation to another by soliciting intergenerational examples of speech. If younger people use a feature of language more than older folks, the feature is most likely on the increase, and if the opposite is true, that older people use a feature more than young people, the feature is losing ground in the language (Trudgill 1983; D. Sankoff 1978; G. Sankoff 1980; Milroy 1980, 1987). From these types of studies, linguists have gleaned which internal and external conditions aid language retention as well as those that most likely accelerate language loss.

Previously, neogrammarian linguists had contended that linguistic change could not be observed, and that only the outcome of linguistic change was available for study (Bloomfield 1933, p. 347; Hockey 1958, pp. 439, 444, both cited in Labov 1986). Labov, Trudgill, D. Sankoff, G. Sankoff, the Milroys, Baugh, and others have successfully used variable rule analysis to measure the effect of various linguistic and social contexts on speech, and to quantify variation and change in different speech communities throughout the world.

Central to variable rule analysis is the concept of the linguistic variable first introduced by Labov. A variable is a linguistic feature that is seen as being sometimes present and sometimes absent in the language of a speaker or speech community. This fluctuation is not always predictable from the structure of the grammar in which it appears. A variable may have two or more variants, which appear neither through obligatory nor optional rule application, but through variable rule application. Variable rule analysis can predict the probability of the occurrence or non-occurrence of the variants based on the frequency of its occurrence in the defined groups of linguistic and social contexts thought to be conditioning that variable. Each factor is assumed to have a fixed effect independent of the other aspects of the environment.

Since Labov introduced variable rule analysis, there have been several generations of statistical computer programs based on his original concepts, each more sophisticated and powerful than the previous one (Cedergren and

Sankoff 1974; Rousseau and Sankoff 1978a, 1978b; Guy 1987; Rand and Sankoff 1988). The computer program Goldvarb was used in this study. Goldvarb is a multiple-regression procedure that uses log likelihood comparisons to estimate the contribution of each specified factor to the application of a rule when all factors are considered simultaneously. In Goldvarb, the contributions of a single factor group are first found, then each factor group is tested to see which one increases the likelihood most significantly (Cedergren and D. Sankoff 1974; Rousseau and D. Sankoff 1978b; G. Sankoff 1980). For this study, the 1988 version of Varbrul, Goldvarb for Macintosh, was used (Rand and Sankoff 1988).

The value of variable rule analysis to the investigation of language is disputed. Some of the dispute centres on the view that in a complicated statistical analysis of group speech, not enough consideration is given to individual characteristics, and that by positing variable rules as a part of a person's linguistic competence, undesirable strains are put on the acquisition device (Bickerton 1971; and others). Romaine (1981, 1984) also questions the general explanatory powers of this type of quantitative analysis (see Dittmar 1976, Chapter 7, for an overview of this criticism).

The greatest value of variable rule analysis is its capacity to give order to linguistic states that previously had been characterized as confusing, unpredictable, and often unimportant. Variable rule analysis has enabled linguists to discover the dynamics of language use within a variety of speech communities and view sound change in progress. But, as Guy (1988, p. 136) has said, "It is only a device (albeit a sophisticated one) for manipulating the data. It does not discern patterns, make generalizations, or explain findings."

THE APPROPRIATENESS OF USING VARIABLE RULE ANALYSIS FOR THIS STUDY

The use of variable rule analysis for the study of Flámæli, the apparent mergers of the front, high (I) and the front, mid (E), and of the front, high, rounded (Y) and the front, mid, rounded (ö) give some order to a very complicated process. This feature has been alternately defined as a single process or many processes. Speakers were found to "merge" one set or both sets. Some "merge" only the long variants. Others also "merge" the short variants (Björn Guðfinnsson 1946, 1964). Others have suggested that Flámæli did not involve merger at all (Þórunn Blöndal 1985). Flámæli may have been used by women more than men, and it spread fast, although how and why it spread have not been determined.

Speculation about the social context of Flámæli, which was widespread in three geographical areas of Iceland until a few decades ago, started only after it no longer existed in Iceland. This dialect feature of Icelandic is the only feature that became stigmatized in Iceland and was eradicated in a few decades through negative public opinion and through the education system.

Variable rule analysis enables us to glean regularity out of the complex linguistic and social context of Flámæli in NA Icelandic, where it is widespread. The results may give us insight into the general nature and spread of Flámæli in Icelandic in Iceland.

CHAPTER 5 **THE GRAMMAR OF NORTH AMERICAN ICELANDIC**

The description of North American Icelandic is presented below with only a rudimentary attempt at analysis in a few instances. A closer examination of the development of one feature of NA Icelandic grammar, Flámæli, is in the remaining chapters. The source for the description in this chapter is my own data collected in 1986, adhering to the strictest possible research methodology (see Chapter 4). All the grammatical phenomena presented are worthy of further study. However, a detailed analysis of every distinguishing feature of NA Icelandic grammar is beyond the scope of this study. It is my hope that the information contained in this chapter may serve as fertile ground for further examination of North American Icelandic and the nature of language development and attrition.

The chapter begins with the discussion of morphology, first verbal morphology and then nominal morphology. The following sections include short treatments of subjunctive mood, pronouns (especially reflexive pronouns), and features of phonetics and phonology. The chapter concludes with a description of NA Icelandic syntax and some final remarks about further research.

MORPHOLOGY

The most studied features of immigrant language attrition in morphology concern changes in case systems of synthetic languages. Scholars (see Chapter 2) have reported on the collapse of accusative and nominative case in Finnish and Pennsylvania Dutch (a variety of German). The loss of dative case and even genitive case has been suggested in Greek and Pennsylvania Dutch. Several of the studies also showed regularizations of verb paradigms and loss of tense distinctions.

North American Icelandic shows surprisingly little attrition in the morphology and although there are indications that there may be some "unrest" in the overt marking of case, there are no speakers who display a consistent loss of these distinctions. The case system of North American Icelandic does not differ in major respects from that of Icelandic in Iceland. The area where attrition is consistently noticeable is in the apparent confusion or unrest in the case assignment by a category of verbs called impersonal verbs or psyche verbs. This unrest is also found in modern Icelandic (Ásta Svavarsdóttir et al. 1984; Jóhannes Gísli Jónsson 1997–98). Some of the simplification processes in both the verbal and the nominal inflections may be a result of semantic and thus categorical shifts in verbs and prepositions that have retained their Icelandic forms but have acquired the functions of their English cognates. Some paradigm simplifications cannot be excluded, either. Over the past decade, there has been a considerable amount of research into the nature of Icelandic inflectional morphology. Although only a few of the studies have dealt with attrition, we have a much better understanding of how Icelandic inflections work today than we did in 1986 when these data were collected (Ásta Svavarsdóttir et al. 1984, Jóhannes Gísli Jónsson (1997–98), Þórhallur Eyþórsson (2000), Maling (2002), and others. Therefore, morphology will receive some attention in the following section.

IMPERSONAL VERBS

Impersonal verbs or psyche verbs are those that assign oblique cases (accusative, dative, or genitive) to their subjects. Impersonal verbs do not agree in person and number with their subjects and are always in the third person. Psyche verbs are rare in the world's languages although there is indication that they did exist in p revious forms of mainland Scandinavian languages and in Hindi (Þórhallur Eyþórsson 2000). As there seems to be change in the nature of these types of verbs in NA Icelandic, and at least one of the phenomena, commonly referred to as þágufallisýki 'Dative Sickness', is also in progress in Icelandic in Iceland, it is tempting to give them a second glance here.

Impersonal verbs can be subdivided according to their thematic roles according to whether they take accusative subjects (about 175) or dative subjects (about 300) (Jóhannes Gísli Jónsson 1997–98; Maling 2002). There is also a handful of verbs with genitive subjects that will not be discussed here. Semantically, subjects of most impersonal verbs are not *doers*, but rather *experiencers* of verbs denoting psychological states, such as feelings, longing, or physical well-being. Verbs like *langa* 'want/long for', *vanta* 'need', *gruna* 'suspect' have subjects in accusative case as seen below in 1. a–c:

1. a. Mig (acc.) langar að læra
      'I long (lit) want to learn'

   b. Jón (acc.) vantar bækur
      'John needs books'

   c. Hana (acc.) grunar að bókinni hafi verið stolið
      'She suspects that the book has been stolen'

Others carry dative case, such as *þykja* 'seem to be/believe to be', *finna* 'perceive/feel', *vera illa við/vera vel við* 'like/dislike', *sýnast* 'to appear to s-e'.

2. a. Mér (dat.) þykir það leitt
      'I think it regretful' (lit.)
      'I regret this'

b. Jóni (dat.) finnst bókin góð
'John thinks the book is good'

c. Henni (dat.) er vel við Jón
'She (dat.) likes John'

d. Mér (dat.) sýnist svarið vera rétt
'I perceive (lit.) the answer to be correct'
'The answer seems correct to me'

There is a widespread tendency for speakers in Iceland to replace accusative subjects with dative subjects to the point that the phenomenon seems to be in the last stages of language change and only maintained by an artificial effort by a few speakers. Eiríkur Rögnvaldsson claims "the language is trying to get rid of the accusative subjects, either by changing them into the nominative or in the dative" (unpublished, undated manuscript, <www.eirikur@hi.is>). The tendency for quirky subjects of impersonal verbs to become either dative or nominative (or personal) is conditioned by two different factors: dative substitution is governed by semantic or thematic roles, while nominative substitution is motivated by syntax (Jóhannes Gísli Jónsson 1997-98; Þórhallur Eyþórsson 2000). Both Þórhallur Eyþórsson and Jóhannes Gísli Jónsson point out, and as the examples below from modern Icelandic suggest, that there are exceptions to this and that Experiencer subjects also can take nominative case. Examples of nominative preference include 3. a–b, where the subject is a theme, and 4. a–c, where the subject is an Experiencer (3a and 4a are considered standard and 4b is an example of dative preference).

3. a. Bátinn (acc.) rak að landi
'The boat drifted ashore'

  b. Báturinn (nom.) rak að landi
'The boat drifted ashore'

4. a. Mig (acc.) dreymdi köttinn
'I dreamt about the cat'

  b. Mér (dat.) dreymdi köttinn
'I dreamt about the cat'

c. Ég (nom.) dreymdi köttinn
   'I dreamt about the cat'

Both phenomena are extensive in the North American Icelandic data, although the discussion below will be limited to Experiencer subjects.

The evolution of unrest in case assignment of impersonal verbs indicates that the Icelandic emigrants must have brought it with them to North America in the late nineteenth century. Halldór Halldórsson (1979) suggests that substituting dative for accusative in subjects of impersonal verbs is a relatively recent phenomenon in the development of Icelandic, with most of the examples dating from the middle of the nineteenth century. Note, though, that his data are based on written documents and it is likely that non-standard forms are found more frequently in spoken than written language.

The most cited study on the unrest and confusion in actual modern Icelandic usage in terms of appropriate case assignment by impersonal verbs is the landmark study reported in Ásta Svavarsdóttir et al. (1984). The goal of the study was to determine the extent of the spread of dative preference or Dative Sickness in the speech of her subjects. By the early 1980s, Dative Sickness had become a marker of sub-standard speech in Iceland and was the subject of debate as to how this could be eradicated. Ásta and her colleagues state that Dative Sickness was so widespread that there were strong arguments for accepting it as standard speech. Ásta found no indication that impersonal verbs in Icelandic are becoming personal (p. 30).

Þórhallur Eyþórsson reports that substitutions of nominative forms for oblique forms can be found as far back as in Old Icelandic, although they are more common in later texts. He refers to this change as Nominative Sickness (2000, pp. 30–31).

The extent of Dative Sickness and Nominative Sickness in the speech of the emigrants to North America is not known, nor the extent of its use in Iceland at the time of the emigrations, but the data from NA Icelandic indicates that this category of verbs with quirky subjects is in the process of undergoing change.

According to Jóhannes Gísli Jónsson (1997–98) and Þórhallur Eyþórsson (2000), Dative Sickness only affects accusative Experiencer subjects (subjects of verbs denoting a psychological state the agent is experiencing—quirky subjects) and Nominative Sickness affects subjects that serve as themes (a theme is the undergoer of the action denoted in the verb as seen in 3. *Bátinn* (*acc.*) *rak að landi* 'The boat drifted ashore'. The boat undergoes the drift. As Þórhallur notes, there are problematic exceptions to this analysis, such as the *dreyma* examples above. The data from NA Icelandic supports the view that this categorization is problematic, as Experiencer verbs in NA Icelandic seem to either assign dative case or nominative where accusative case is found in the standard variety.

In examples 5. a–b, the verb *langa* has retained its meaning in NA Icelandic and should retain the accusative subject, but the subjects have dative case, which is in line with the phenomenon found in Iceland. This is an instance of Dative Sickness. The 'standard' Icelandic form is given in brackets.

langa

5. a. *henni* (*dat.*) *langaði*
   [hana (acc.) langaði]
   'she wanted'

   b. *mér* (*dat.*) *langar* til að tefla
   [mig (acc.) langar til að tefla]
   'I want to play chess'

In examples 6. a–c, 'want' has various meanings but all examples have the dative subject rather than the accusative.

6. a. svo *vantaði henni* (dat.) náttúrulega að vita hvað það væri
   [svo langaði *hana* (*acc.*) náttúrulega að vita hvað það væri]
   'of course she wanted to know what it was'

   b. … *þeim vantaði* að vera þar sem var nógu mikill viður
   [*þeir þurftu* að vera (vildu vera?) þar sem var nógu mikill viður]
   '… they needed to be where there was enough wood'

c. ... hvort það var nokkuð sérstakt sem mér vantaði
[hvort það væri nokkuð sérstakt sem mig vantaði]
'...if there was anything in particular that I needed'

In the following examples from NA Icelandic, the verbs have become regular personal verbs and assign nominative case to their subjects. All the subjects below are Experiencer subjects and do not fall into the category of subjects associated with Nominative Sickness above; i.e., where the subject is a theme. The phrases *að vera vel við* 'to like' or *að vera illa við* 'to dislike' have dative Experiencer subjects in Icelandic. In this case one would expect few mistakes, given the tendency to use dative above, but the preferred case is nominative and the subject and verb also agree in number as in personal verbs. In the first example (7a), the subject is in plural nominative and the verb agrees. In standard Icelandic, the subject is in dative:

7. a. ... *þeir* (*nom. plur.*)*voru* (past plur.) illa við úlfana
[*þeim* (*dat. plur*) *var* (*past sg.*) illa við úlfana]
'they did not like the wolves'

b. ... *pabbi* (nom.) var nú alltaf illa við það
[*pabba* (dat.) var nú alltaf illa við það]
'dad never liked that'

c. ... *ég* (nom.) var alltaf illa við fisk
[*mér* (dat.) var illa við fisk]
'I never liked fish much'

The verb *þykir* 'seem to be/believe to be' also has dative subject but here again the preference for nominative subject is clear. In this case it seems that the case preference is different, but not that the verb is becoming personal. This is seen in sentence 8a, which has a double subject, yet the verb retains the sg. form, where one might expect a plural form consistent with personal verbs. Of course, it is also possible that this speaker is just making a production error. In the last example, 8c, the subject of the main clause is in dative, but the subject of the subordinate clause is in nominative. Perhaps the reason is that names are normally not inflected and thus the pronoun isn't, either.

8. a. ... *mamma og pabbi* (nom.) þótti voða gaman
   [mömmu og pabba (dat.) þótti voða gaman]
   'mom and dad liked it'

   b. ... *unga fólkið* (*nom.*) þótti þetta erfitt
   [... unga fólkinu (dat.) þótti þetta erfitt]
   '... the young people thought it was difficult'

   c. ... *þykir honum* (dat.) *gaman að þessu, hann Bessason* (*nom.*)
   [... þykir honum (dat.) gaman að þessu, honum (dat), Bessasyni (dat.)]
   '... does he seem to like that, he, Bessason'

There seems to be a third process ongoing, as some of the verbs seem to have undergone a relexification and categorical shift, most likely as a result of transfer from English. This transfer is twofold. The first involves the North American Icelandic verb *vanta* 'need', which has almost entirely been given the function of its English cognate 'want' and is used as such to cover the meaning of Icelandic verbs like the impersonal: *vanta*, which has an accusative subject, *skorta*, also with accusative subject, and also regular personal verbs like *þurfa, þarfnast*, and *vilja*, all with nominative subjects. The meaning of the above-mentioned verbs has been collapsed into the meaning of English 'want' and relexified into the personal verb *vanta* in NA Icelandic.

In sentences 9 to 11, the verb 'want' overtly represented by *vanta* has the semantic function or meaning of *vilja* in Icelandic. *Vilja* is a regular verb with a nominative subject. In Icelandic *vanta* assigns accusative case. The case assignment for the verb *vanta* thus covers the meaning of both *vilja* and *vanta* in Icelandic.

9. *ég* (*nom.*) mundi ekki *vanta* að vera ... (NAI)
   [*ég* (*nom.*) mundi ekki *vilja* vera] (I)
   'I would not want to be'

10. maður gerði það sem *maður* (*nom.*) *vantaði* (NAI)
    [maður gerði það sem *maður* (*nom.*) *vildi*] (I)
    'one just did what one wanted'

11.   *hún (nom.) vantaði* aldrei að gleyma að tala íslensku
      [*hún (nom.) vildi* aldrei gleyma að tala íslensku]
      'she never wanted to forget how to speak Icelandic'

In sentence 12, 'want' has the meaning of *langa* 'would like to', which is an impersonal verb with an accusative subject but has a narrower meaning in Icelandic than 'want' does in English.

12.   *mig (acc.) vantaði* svo mikið að baka vínartertu
      [mig (acc) *langaði* svo mikið að baka vínartertu]
      'I wanted so much to bake a vinarterta'

Sýnast is a 'double' verb or a reflexive verb and means 'something seems like s-g to the speaker'. For example: *mér sýnist hann vera veikur* 'It seems to me like he is ill' but not 'he seems ill'. The subject of *sýnast* is the Experiencer and is assigned dative case to the subject. The meaning in NA Icelandic has almost completely shifted from the first-person perspective of the Icelandic form to the second- or third-person perspective as in English and appears in nominative form; i.e., 'he looks like'. Very few instances of the standard Icelandic form are found in the data.

13. a.   *hann sýnist* ekki vera laupa
        [mér sýnist hann vera að hlaupa]
        'he doesn't look like he is running'

    b.   *Það sýndist* ekki vera sérstaklega merkilegar búskaparaðferðir hjá karlgreyinu ...

        [Mér sýndist búskaparaðferðirnar ekki sérstaklega merkilegar hjá karlgreyinu ...]

        'It didn't look like the poor old guy's farming methods were that impressive'

    c.   ... *þetta sýndist* allt öðruvísi
        [...mér sýnist þetta]
        'it seemed totally different'

d. *Þær sýnast* alltaf koma upp
   [...mér sýnist þær]
   'They always seem to come up'

In 13. a–d, there may be confusion or collapse with the verb *virðast* 'seems' as in 'he seems', which, if substituted for *sýnast*, would be appropriate in those contexts.

The results suggest that the gradual change in impersonal verbs with quirky subjects in North American Icelandic is caused by three processes interacting. The first process is a preference for dative subjects where accusative subjects are appropriate. This process is found in all varieties of Icelandic in Iceland. There are two processes caused by transfer from English: a semantic shift, which causes a recategorization of impersonal verbs as personal verbs, and the relexification of several verbs into one; e.g., *vanta* 'want', which has now become a personal verb in North American Icelandic.

The cause of linguistic change and the mechanisms by which languages are simplified or die out are not easily understood. Studies in case attrition in immigrant languages in the US have generally been descriptive and have offered little in terms of explanations for the processes observed (e.g. Kartunnen 1977 [Finnish]; Anderson and Martin 1976 [German] cited in Lambert and Freed 1982; and others). Language attrition research has been dominated by Roman Jacobson's (1968) regression hypothesis, which states that the process of language attrition is the reverse of language acquisition or language learning process. Regression presupposes gradualness and a more or less fixed sequence/order in acquisition and loss. Jordens at al. (1989) assume that "if language attrition were a process of regression, we should expect a gradual disappearance of the differentiation of the morphological system. First, a reduction from a case system with three options—nominative, dative, and accusative, to a two-state system—nominative and accusative, will take place" (p. 180). This is not the case for impersonal verbs in North American Icelandic.

There is very little research testing the regression hypothesis (Jordens et al. 1989, p. 180). Also, current studies in second language acquisition and sociolinguistics assume a complexity in the acquisition process that includes factors such as transfer, markedness, and developmental processes that pose problems for an examination of gradualness in la nguage evolution. According to Jordens et al. (1989) case marking in German meets the condition of gradualness and a more or less fixed order of acquisition, but his study of attrition in German case marking by German expatriates in Holland indicated that mistakes will occur as a result of the speaker's tendency to establish a one-to-one correspondence between cognitive function and morphological case assignment. This is when case marking ceases to be based on grammatical functions and becomes connected more directly to underlying semantics or meaning. This is apparent in North American Icelandic as the categorical shift from the marked impersonal verbs with oblique cases that function as subjects are switched to the unmarked nominative case more commonly assigned to subjects (the doer) of sentences.

The results reported here support an overall thesis that speakers might try to reconcile the cognitive and grammatical function in case assignment. However, the results also suggest a more complex process wherein three factors interact. Two of these processes are possibly the result of transfer from the dominant language; one due to relexification and subsequent recategorization of impersonal verbs as personal, the other due to semantic shift and recategorization as impersonal verbs become personal, although this may be due to a larger change in progress in the language. The third process is the dative preference found also in Icelandic in Iceland and may be a simplification effort; i.e., the effort to reduce the number of variables available to the speakers in case assignment of impersonal verbs. The next obvious step is to place the data described above into the theoretical context of the nature and development of impersonal verbs in general. This is beyond the scope of this description.

THE TENDENCY TOWARDS REGULARIZATION OF THE VERB PARADIGMS

This section presents several examples of regularization found in NA Icelandic verb morphology. Verbs in Icelandic are divided into two main classes, according to the conjugation patterns they follow. There are twenty-four conjugation classes in all, but, for our purposes, a description of the weak and strong classes suffices. (Just how many conjugation classes there are varies from one grammar book to another.) Weak verbs are those whose past tense is formed by adding a suffix that consists of an ð, t, or d + vowel—four classes in all. Examples: *kalla* (inf.) -*kallaði* (past), *heyra* (inf.) -*heyrði* (past), and *telja* (inf.) -*taldi* where the root vowel must also be changed. The strong verb classes have irregular conjugation paradigms and consist of much fewer verbs than the weak class. The strong conjugation paradigms are characterized by the various vowel changes in the verb roots. Note that the terms *regular* and *irregular* classes are purposely avoided in this context, as they do not neatly apply to verb conjugation classes in Icelandic. Icelandic verbs can have regular endings, but also vowel alternations in the stems.

In the NA Icelandic data, the majority of borrowed verbs are conjugated according to the most common verb class exemplified by *kalla-kallaði*. In addition, strong verbs are conjugated as weak verbs, weak verbs are recategorized, and strong verb paradigms are simplified. None of these were extensive in the data but need further study. A few examples are included here for illustration (standard form in parentheses).

Strong conjugation paradigms become weak (regular) conjugation paradigms

14. maður sem *hlaðaði* (hlóð) því
     'a man who *loaded* it'

15. hann *kveðaði* (kvað)
     'he *recited*'

16. þau *hlaupuðu* (hlupu) framhjá
     'they *ran* past'

17. það voru menn sem *bjóu* (bjuggu) þetta til
     'there were men who *made* this'

18. ég *róaði* yfir vatnið (réri)
     'I *rowed* across the lake'

Simplification of the verb paradigm

There are a few examples of loss of umlaut; i.e., verbs that have alternations between (a)-(ö), (a)-(E). Note that if this were merely a case of phonetic change—i.e., unrounding of front rounded /ö/—the sound would become /E/

as in *kvertuðu /kvERtYðY/. This is not the case. The forms in the following examples have the underlying sound /a/ in all forms in the paradigm:

19. þeir *kvartuðu* (kvörtuðu) undan því
     'they *complained* about it'

20. stúlkurnar sem þær voru að leika sér við *taluðu* ekkert nema íslensku.
     'the girls whom they were playing with *spoke* only Icelandic'

21. þeir *kalluðu* (kölluðu) mig Gallann
     'they *called* me "the Gall"'

Regularization and simplification are common in language attrition and this data warrants further scrutiny for the purpose of shedding light on the nature of those processes.

NOUNS

Icelandic nouns are difficult to categorize according to inflectional patterns. Nouns in Icelandic have four cases: nominative, accusative, dative, and genitive; and three grammatical genders: masculine, feminine, and neuter. Nouns get assigned case by either verbs or by prepositions. In the NA Icelandic data, there was some confusion in terms of case assignment, or at least overt marking of case, although this did not seem regular or consistent upon preliminary analysis. Recall that proper names are an exception to this, as they are usually not declined in NA Icelandic (see previous chapter for discussion).

Case Assignment of Nouns by Verbs

Below are some examples of 'confusion' in case assignment by verbs. The 'appropriate' form of the noun is in brackets.

22. F hljóp inn og sagði okkur (acc/dat.), ég (nom.) og indjánann (acc.) og annar maður (nom.) sem var þar

    [F hljóp inn og sagði okkur (dat.), mér (dat.) og indjánanum (dat.) og öðrum manni (dat.) sem var þar ...]
    'F ran inside and told us, I and the Indian and another man who was there.'

23. sonurinn kynnti *henni* (dat.) þessum manni
    [sonurinn kynnti hana (acc.) fyrir þessum manni]
    'the son introduced her to this man'

24. uppeldissystir *faðir* (nom.) míns
    [uppeldissystir föður (gen.) míns]
    'my father's stepsister'

25. þeir voru vanir *vatn* (nom.? acc.?)
    [þeir voru vanir vatni (dat.)]
    'they were used to water'

Case Assigned by Prepositions

Case assignment by preposition has undergone some attrition in NA Icelandic morphology. The most consistent regularity is that proper names of people and places are always in the nominative case, regardless of the preposition that precedes them. In other instances, case assignment by prepositions needs much closer scrutiny, as it seems that here, as in the impersonal verb category discussed previously, there is interplay of transfer of English meaning onto the Icelandic form, collapse of two or more prepositions into one, and other interesting phenomena. The NA Icelandic preposition *fyrir* functions in many cases like the English 'for' and includes the meaning of Icelandic *í* in some cases. The Icelandic *fyrir* can have the same meaning as 'for' but not always. Similarly, the Icelandic preposition *af* functions as English 'of'. Although there is some attrition in this category, the influence of semantic transfer should not be ignored, nor the possibility of case syncretism, and waits further study. Below are a few examples of case assignment by preposition in NA Icelandic.

af: In the sentences below, *af* should assign dative case.

26. ... eins og þeir gátu borðað af fisk_ (acc.?)
    [eins og þeir gátu borðað af fiski (dat.)]
    '... all they could eat of fish'

27. svona hálfa teskeið af lyftiduft_ (nom. acc.*)
    [svona hálfa teskeið af lyftidufti (dat.)]
    'about a half a teaspoon of baking soda'

til: The preposition *til* 'to' assigns genitive case.

28. frá þremur (dat.) til fjórum (dat.) eða fimm mílur (nom./acc.)
    [frá þremur til fjögurra (gen.) eða fimm mílna (gen.)]
    'from three to four or five miles'

yfir: In sentences 29–30, *yfir* assigns accusative case in standard Icelandic but the speakers used dative.

29. ég man nú ekki nafnið yfir þessu (dat.)
    [ég man nú ekki nafnið yfir þetta (acc.)]
    'I don't remember the name for this'

30. ... ekkert orð yfir því (dat.)
    [... ekkert orð yfir það (acc.)]
    '... no word for this'

með: The preposition *með* assigns dative case in standard Icelandic in sentences 31–32 and accusative case in sentence 33.

31. kjóll með *tölur* (nom.? acc.?) á
    [kjóll með tölum (dat.) á]
    'a dress with buttons on'

32. komdu *með klárann*
    [komdu með klárinn (acc.)]
    'bring the horse'

33. alltaf kynnt með við (acc.*)
    [alltaf kynnt með viði (dat.)]
    'always heated with wood'

*also found in modern Icelandic and referred to as the new dative

á:

34. ... að horfa á *þeir* (nom. plur.)
    [... að horfa á þá (acc. plur.)]
    '... to watch them'

35. það var í allt vondur tími *á árið* (acc.)
    [það var vondur tími á árinu (dat.)]
    'it was, all in all, a bad time of year'

36. ... moka skít *á vetrin*
    [... moka skít á veturna]
    '... shovel manure in winter'

There are numerous examples in the data of the construction *á vetrin*. The modern standard form is *á veturna*. The neutral form *vetrin* was found in some dialects of Icelandic but was not common. It seems that this form has become preferred in NA Icelandic, possibly by analogy. The words for the other three seasons of the year—*vor, sumar, haust*—all belong to the same conjugation class, which is different from the class *vetur*. With the preposition *á* they take the following forms: *á vorin, á sumrin, á haustin*, hence we get *á vetrin*, which in modern Icelandic would be *á veturna*.

í: Examples 37–38 show *í* being used as English *in*:

37. hún spurði mig *í ensku*
    [hún spurði mig á ensku]
    'she asked me in English'

38. þegar ég fór *í áttatíu og tvö*
    [þegar ég fór áttatíu og tvö]
    'when I went in eighty-two'

In examples 39–40, *í* assigns nominative or accusative cases rather than the dative case, as in standard Icelandic.

39. ég var að vinna í kjötmarkað_(acc.*)
    [ég var að vinna í kjötmarkaði (dat.)]
    'I was working at a meat market'

40. við lentum í *slys* (nom.? acc.? new dat.?)
    [við lentum í slysi (dat.)]
    'we had an accident'

fyrir: This preposition has almost entirely taken over the function of the English preposition *for*, as the following sentences illustrate:

41. þegar ég var búin með University þá fór ég til Evrópu *fyrir tíma*
    [þegar ég var búin með University þá fór ég til Evrópu *um tíma*]
    'when I had finished university then I went to Europe for a while'

42. ég lenti á spítala *fyrir tvær nætur*
    [ég lenti á spítala í tvær nætur]
    'I was in the hospital for two nights'

In examples 43 and 44, *fyrir* assigns a different case than is customary in modern Icelandic:

43. ... búið að gera nýjar blæjur *fyrir gluggunum* (dat.)
    [... búið að gera ný gluggatjöld fyrir gluggana (acc.)]
    '... had made new curtains for the windows'

44. það var ákaflega mikil hjálp *fyrir þeim*
    [það var ákaflega mikil hjálp fyrir þau]
    'that was a great help to them'

Needless to say, there is more here than meets the eye and the issue of change in prepositions, a closed morphological class, needs further study.

Archaic Endings

In the NA Icelandic data, there are many examples of inflectional markings that are no longer considered standard Icelandic (as seen in brackets) but were common in earlier forms of Icelandic. Here may be another instance of 'unrest' in the language as forms like *komustum* (46) are reportedly found in the speech of young speakers in Iceland (Margrét Jónsdóttir, personal communication). Here are some examples:

45. þetta brúka lækn*irarnir* (nom. plur. def. art.)
    [þetta nota lækn*arnir*]
    'this is used by doctors'

46. við *komustum* ekki aftur á ísinn fyrr en eftir jól
    [við *komumst* ekki aftur á ísinn fyrr en eftir jól]
    'we couldn't get back on the ice until after Christmas'

47. ef við *mætustum*, (1. pers. plur. refl.) eldri systkinin, þá tölum við íslensku
    [ef við *hittumst*?, eldri systkinin, þá tölum við íslensku]
    'when we meet, the older siblings, then we speak Icelandic'

48. við ól*ustum* upp (1. pers. plur. refl.) ...
    [við ól*umst* upp ...]
    'we grew up ...'

49. við útskrifu*ðustum*
    [við útskrifu*ðumst*]
    'we graduated'

Clearly, North American Icelandic has not been influenced by the language purism policies of twentieth-century Iceland.

SUBJUNCTIVE

Haraldur Bessason (1984a, 1984b) reports a loss of subjunctive by many speakers of NA Icelandic. This study revealed some loss of subjunctive but sometimes only in the overt marking of subjunctive. Speakers would often substitute the Icelandic forms with the word *mundi*, which is a direct transfer from English 'would'. Sentences 50 and 51 are examples of this (subjunctive forms in Icelandic are in brackets).

50. hann skrifaði þeim að hann *mundi* ekki vera kallaður í herinn
    [hann skrifaði þeim að hann *yrði ekki* kallaður í herinn]
    'he wrote to them that he would not be called into the army'

51. ég *mundi* ekki vanta að vera
    [ég *vildi* ekki vera]
    'I would not want to be'

In most cases the subjunctive mood is replaced by verbs in indicative mood, as in examples 52–57 below.

52. þeir vildu nú ekki trúa mér að ég *kom* (kæmi) frá Kanada
    'they would not believe me that I came from Canada'
53. ég hélt að það *var* (væri) miklu kaldara
    'I thought it was much colder'
54. sumir sögðu að hann *hafði* (hefði) átt að keppa
    'some said that he should have competed'
55. ef ég *hafði* (hefði) fólk þar sem er skylt okkur, *ég mundi* (færi) kannski *fara*
    'if we had relatives there, I might go'
56. hvort það *var* (væri) nokkuð sérstakt sem mér vantaði
    'if there was anything in particular that I needed'
57. þau *höfðu* (hefðu) öll farið með því
    'they would have all gone with it'

This area needs further scrutiny before any conclusions can be drawn about the attrition of subjunctive.

PHONETICS AND PHONOLOGY

With the exception of three or four of the oldest speakers, all the informants spoke Icelandic with different degrees of American or Canadian accents. The accents were not reminiscent of speakers of Icelandic as a foreign language, but, rather, had a fluency and accuracy in terms of how they hit the phonetic targets of speakers struggling with a limited range of registers and vocabulary. To a native speaker of Icelandic, they spoke not like speakers who had learned Icelandic as a foreign language and had a different first language, but more like they did, in fact, speak a different kind of Icelandic. Informants' demeanour was that of Icelanders when they spoke Icelandic. This is best exemplified by the familiarity and ease with which most of the informants used Icelandic greeting conventions and the common Icelandic practice of starting an initial conversation by finding out *hverra manna* I was or establishing a common acquaintance or link between the interlocutors. A literal English translation of the term *hverra manna ertu?* is 'of what people are you?' What ensues is a co mplex interchange of questions back and forth between the interlocutors until a common connection has been established between the speakers and the new person's familial or geographical affiliations identified. In the case of NA Icelandic, I was usually first asked whether I had relatives in the immigrant communities—whether any of my 'people' had emigrated. When I replied in the negative, I was asked where I was from in Iceland—hoping perhaps that they could make a geographical connection. Since I grew up in an area in Iceland that saw little emigration, this often proved unfruitful. The final resort was usually to connect me to well-known Icelanders in Winnipeg who were affiliated with the university where I had my base. Once the connection was made, the conversation could move on to the business at hand. By way of contrast, a learner of Icelandic as a foreign language once attempted to establish this connection by using the direct approach by asking me straight out, in good Icelandic, whom I knew. After some bewilderment, I understood this to be an effort to establish a connection and was able to guide the person towards the appropriate manner to connect the interlocutors.

The most pronounced characteristic of the North American Icelandic accent is the merger of the high vowel /I/ and the mid vowel /E/ and the merger of their front rounded counterparts /Y/ and /ö/, popularly known as Flámæli. This feature is the focus of the next chapters. Below is a short description of other prominent phonetic and phonological characteristics of North American Icelandic.

Dialect Levelling

Some dialect levelling is apparent in NA Icelandic in that there seems to be a reduction or attrition of certain Icelandic dialect variants and an increase in spread of other variants (variation in Icelandic is almost exclusively phonetic or phonological). Only one dialect variant was absent in the data. This was the monophthongal pronunciation before velar nasals found in the western fjords region of Iceland; e.g. *langur* [laŋkYR] instead of the more common [lauŋkYR].

None of the speakers seemed, consistently and regularly, to use features of a single variety. The other case was much more frequent; i.e., informants blended features from different dialects into a hybrid dialect not found in Iceland. The same speaker might thus have in his speech features characteristic of several different regions in Iceland. The same individual could have Harðmæli (aspiration of intervocalic stops), which is c haracteristic of northern Iceland, and Flámæli (merging of [I] and [E] or [Y] and [ö]), which are features of speech mainly in s outhern and eastern parts of Iceland. In Iceland one would normally not find these features in the speech of the same speaker. This impression is su pported by Clausing (1984) in his st udy of dialect levelling in NA Icelandic.

Many features seem to have lexicalized in that the majority of informants had Flámæli in words such as *spil* [spI:l] 'cards' on the picture identification task, pronouncing it as [spE:l], a nd other words such as *pípa* 'pipe' were consistently pronounced with the intervocalic consonant aspirated [pipha] as in northern speech (Harðmæli).

Simplification of Initial Consonant Clusters

Simplification of consonant clusters *hr-, hl-, hn-,* and *hv-* in initial position is widespread in NA Icelandic. These clusters seem to be treated as a class and are simplified to voiced *r-, l-, n-,* and *v-*. In most modern dialects of Icelandic, *hr-, hl-, hn-* are voiceless and *hv-* is pronounced as *kv-*. Initial consonant clusters *kv-* are common in English in words such as question, queen etc. Yet in NA Icelandic the initial *h+ r, l, n,* and *(k)v,* respectively, is treated as one process and the simplification to voiced *r, l,* and *n* is extended to *v* as well. Thus *hrædd* 'scared', *hræðileg* 'terrible', *hreinsa* 'to clean' become *ræddi, ræðileg,* and *reinsa; hlaupa* 'run', *hnota* 'wood knot', *hnepptur* 'buttoned' become *laupa, nota, nepptur*. Also, *hvalur* 'whale', *hvítt* 'white', *hvasst* 'windy', *hvolpur* 'puppy' become *valur, vítt, vasst, volpur,* or *kolpur*. There are also examples of *xv-* [xvas:t], [xvituR], which is characteristic of speech in southeastern parts of Iceland.

This phenomenon needs further scrutiny as the continuum *kv- -> xv- ->v-* came up in the speech of three generations within the same family. Simplification was in a f ew examples generalized to *kvöld*, which in NA Icelandic is pronounced *völd*.

Unrounding of (ö) to (E)

The unrounding of front rounded (ö) is very common in NA Icelandic, probably due to direct influence from English, which has no front rounded equivalent. These forms are also found in modern Icelandic, although they are rare today. They may have been more commonplace in earlier forms of Icelandic, which could be another explanation for their frequency in NA Icelandic. Examples:

Hnettur	instead of hnöttur	globe
vekva	instead of vökva	water
exum	" öxum	axes
mje	" mjö(g)	very
kjet	" kjöt	meat
kekur	" kökur	cakes

One informant seemed to have a half-rounded /E/.

Disappearance of Voiced Velar Fricative

In Icelandic (g) in orthography is realized as a voiced velar fricative /γ/ intervocalically and following a vowel word finally. This voiced velar fricative is disappearing in NA Icelandic, especially in the speech of many speakers of Icelandic in N orth Dakota. Accordingly, words like *sög* (sö:ā) 'a saw' and *flugur* (flY:γYr) are pronounced (sö:), (flY:Yr). The voiced velar fricative is always found in some common words such as *eiga* 'own' and *augu* 'eyes' in the data.

SYNTAX

There is very little change apparent in the syntax of NA Icelandic. There seems to be a slight increase in use of prepositional phrases instead of inflections (examples 58–60) a nd other constructions characteristic of changes from synthetic to analytic language characteristics. But this is tr ue of modern Icelandic as well.

58. þetta var sent á hverjum þremur, fjórum dögum
 [þetta var sent þriðja, fjórða hvern dag]
 'this was sent every three, four days'

59. kannski við höfum gefið það bara til indjánanna.
 [kannski höfum við gefið indjánunum það]
 'perhaps we just gave it to the Indians'

60. flestir af krökkunum töluðu allir íslensku
 [flestir krakkanna töluðu íslensku]
 'most of the kids all spoke Icelandic'

Sometimes English constructions such as do-support are transferred to Icelandic as in examples 61–62. The auxiliary 'do' is translated into Icelandic as *gera* 'to make/ to do'. In Icelandic *gera* is a transitive verb that requires a following np. In NA Icelandic the function of *gera* is extended and is used like *do*, for example in sentence tags.

61. ... við M gerum __
 [... við M gerum það]
 '... M and I do'

62. hún vildi ekki really tala við hana, en hún gerði __
 [hún vildi ekki really tala við hana, en hún gerði það]
 'she didn't really want to talk to her but she did'

Adverb Placement

The most prominent change in the syntax of NA Icelandic is in adverb placement. It is tempting to explain this as the transfer of the English rules of adverb placement to Icelandic, but adverb placement is a complex phenomenon that is not well understood. Distribution of adverbs varies cross-linguistically with subcategories of adverbs behaving differently within the same language. Below are some examples of adverb placement in NA Icelandic. In sentences 63–64 the adverb precedes the verb in NA Icelandic as in English. In standard Icelandic the adverb follows the verb.

63. hún var fjórtán ára þegar hún *fyrst* kom frá Kanada
 [hún var fjórtán ára þegar hún kom *fyrst* frá Kanada]
 'she was fourteen when she first came from Canada'

64. Ef ég hafði fólk þar sem er skylt okkur, ég mundi kannski fara
 [Ef ég ætti ættingja þar, mundi ég kannski fara/færi ég kannski]
 'If I had people there who were related to us, maybe I might go'

Examples 65-69 co ntain adverbs that could be categorized as s entence adverbs. They can either follow the verb or appear sentence initially, in which case the subject and verb are inverted. In the NA Icelandic examples below, adverbs are placed according to English distribution rules. They either precede the verb or, if they appear sentence initially, the subject and verb are not inverted.

65. Doris *stundum* talar íslensku
 [Doris talar *stundum* íslensku]
 'Doris sometimes speaks Icelandic'

66. við *aldrei* notuðum ...
 [við notuðum aldrei ...]
 'we never used ...'

67. *stundum* ég hugsa um það
 [ég hugsa stundum um það]
 or [stundum hugsa ég um það]
 'sometimes I think about'

68. *fyrst* við fiskuðum í norðurendanum
 [við fiskuðum fyrst í norðurendanum]
 or [fyrst fiskuðum við í norðurendanum]
 'first we fished in the north end'

69. *kannski* við höfum gefið það bara til indjánanna.
 [kannski höfum við gefið indjánunum það]
 or [við höfum kannski gefið indjánunum það]
 'perhaps we just gave it to the Indians'

'It Is'

One of the more curious transfers from English is the borrowing and translation of the phrase 'It is'. In English the verb 'to be' always agrees with the dummy subject 'It' and this is also the case for NA Icelandic. This translation has replaced the Icelandic expression where the verb agrees with the actual subject and not 'It'. 'It is' and *það er* have overlapping functions in English and Icelandic. In NA Icelandic *það er* seems to function in all cases as 'It is'. The verb agrees with dummy deictic subject 'it' even in functions where there is no correspondence between the two languages. Some of the examples presented below are in passive voice and all need further investigation.

70. Það er_ alltaf fimm spil
    [það eru alltaf fimm spil]
    'There are always five cards'

71. það var sett_ ís í kringum þetta
    [það var settur ís í kringum þetta]
    'ice was put around it'

72. það var brúkaðir hundar
    [það voru brúkaðir hundar]
    'dogs were used'

73. það var mest talað íslenska
    [það var aðallega töluð íslenska]
    'Icelandic was mostly spoken'

CONCLUSION

Providing a description of North American Icelandic, the only variety of Icelandic spoken outside Iceland, is a worthy undertaking that may have some historical significance. Closer examination of the data with a view to placing it within the larger theoretical discussion of the evolution of Icelandic, in the past and in the future, given the close proximity with English, may prove fruitful. For example: what features of Icelandic are likely to undergo change and in what manner? The development of impersonal verbs, prepositions, and the distribution of adverbs have theoretical implications that should be explored further. Finally, closer inspection of this data may shed some light on the process of learning Icelandic as a second language. Is there, in fact, a connection between how languages are learned and how they are forgotten? Are the features that are lost first the ones that are learned last and do they pose the greatest difficulty for learners of Icelandic as a second language, as the regression hypothesis suggests? What, if anything, can the fact that English loanwords were assigned gender in NA Icelandic with some consistency tell us about how adult foreign language learners assign grammatical gender to Icelandic words? These are all broad theoretical questions, which inherently contain numerous other questions. It is my hope that the data presented above will prove to be fertile ground for further study of North American Icelandic.

CHAPTER 6 **PERCEIVED VOWEL MERGERS: IDENTIFICATION OF THE VARIABLES**

The apparent mergers of the high, front, lax vowel (I), and the mid front vowel (E) on the one hand, and the high, front, lax, rounded vowel (Y) and mid, front, rounded vowel (ö) on the other hand, traditionally referred to as Flámæli, were found in three regional dialects of Icelandic up until the last few decades.

Between 5000 and 6000 of the more than 14,000 Icelandic emigrants to North America in the late nineteenth century were from the regions where Flámæli was prevalent, according to Júníus Kristjánsson's table (see Table 2, Chapter 1). They probably did not all have Flámæli in their speech, however, and it is impossible to know exactly how many did. We do know that Flámæli has spread throughout the speech of the immigrants and is one of the more salient characteristics of North American Icelandic. Studying Flámæli in North American Icelandic provides a uniq ue opportunity to study this apparent sound change in progress.

This chapter presents the linguistic context of Flámæli and defines the relevant linguistic factors that are thought to affect the occurrence of Flámæli.

This is followed by a discussion of Flámæli in its social context, and a definition of the social factors that are believed to constrain or encourage Flámæli. Finally, this study is placed within the general framework of the nature of vowel mergers and apparent mergers.

THE LINGUISTIC CONTEXT OF THE LOWERING OF [I] AND [Y] AND THE RAISING OF [E] AND [Ö] IN ICELANDIC

The Icelandic vowel system has eight vowels: five front vowels, unrounded (i, I, E) and rounded (Y, ö); and three back vowels, unrounded (a) and rounded (o, u). There are also five diphthongs: (Ey, ay, au, öy, ou). These vowels can be either long or short, depending on syllable weight and stress. This vowel inventory is shared by most speakers of modern Icelandic. That was not always the case. The most extensive study of dialects in Iceland (prior to RÍN, conducted in the 1980s) was conducted by Björn Guðfinnsson in the 1940s. Björn Guðfinnsson found a widespread tendency among speakers in three geographical areas to "merge" two sets of the front vowels (I) and (E), and (Y) and (ö), and, more precisely, to lower (I) and (Y), and raise (E) and (ö) in their long variants to form intermediate vowels. See Figure 2.

FIGURE 2
The Icelandic Vowel System

The arrows indicate the directions of the apparent mergers.

	front		back
	-round	+round	+round
high	i		u
	I ↕	Y ↕	
mid	E	ö	o
low			a

The result of these phenomena is that words such as the ones below are perceived as homonyms:

[skI:R]	a milk product	and	[skE:R]	islet
[vI:ðYR]	wood	and	[vE:ðYR]	weather
[flY:γYR]	flies	and	[flö:γYR]	tiles

Björn Guðfinnsson also found a few examples of Flámæli in the short variants forming homonyms like the following:

[kInt]	sheep	and	[kEnt]	feeling
[lYnt]	mood	and	[lönt]	countries

By far the most common form of Flámæli was the lowering of [I], then [Y], then the raising of [E] and [ö], respectively. Because Björn Guðfinnsson did not believe that the vowels were completely merged, he represents the raised and lowered variants with separate symbols. This tradition is followed in this study. The following symbols are used to represent Flámæli:

[I] regular vowel	[I]	lowered variant
[Y] " "	[Y]	" "
[E] " "	[E]	raised "
[ö] " "	[ö]	" "

The lowered variants represent any possible degree of lowering and the raised variants represent any degree of raising.

Before discussing the linguistic and social factors that are thought to influence Flámæli in NA Icelandic, some clarifications of the definition of Flámæli are in order. Following the practice of Þórunn Blöndal (1985) and Höskuldur Þráinsson and Kristján Árnason (1984), the term Flámæli is used for the apparent mergers described above, and also in those instances where there might be diphthongization involved or a version of Flámæli that Björn Guðfinnsson calls 'slappmæli' (sloppy speech); i.e., the vowels are not raised enough or lowered enough to be considered true Flámæli. Both phenomena are important to the investigation of Flámæli, but the explanation of just how the different aspects of Flámæli are connected has so far eluded investigators.

Björn Guðfinnsson (1964), Höskuldur Þráinsson and Kristján Árnason (1984), and Þórunn Blöndal (1985) refer to a small number of their informants who seem to have neither clear Flámæli nor the standard forms. Þórunn Blöndal opted to include those with Flámæli, as the difference between the two "types" of Flámæli did not warrant categorizing them separately. About 10% of Björn Guðfinnsson's informants are in this 'intermediate group'. This group included those who seemed to have diphthongization of the Flámæli vowels and unclear Flámæli. Björn Guðfinnsson gives this explanation for grouping the two together separately from Flámæli;

> Í þessum hópi eru mjög margir þeirra sem hafa einhvern tíma verið flámæltir og leitast við að venja sig af þessum framburði en ekki tekist til hlítar. Enn eru í þessum flokki þeir er hafa óvenjulegt og grunns- amlegt tvíhljóðaskrið í fyrrgreindum sérhljóðum. Nú er það alkunna meðal hljóðfræðinga að tvíhl jóðaskriðs gætir í flestum löngum sérhljóðum í íslen sku í f ramburði fjölmargra réttmæltra manna. Getur stundum verið vafamál hvort þetta skrið er eðlilegt eða flámæli á byrjunarstigi. (p. 36)

> 'In this group there are many who at one time had Flá mæli and are trying to change their pronunciation without success. Also included in this group are those who suspiciously diphthongize these particular vowels. It is common knowledge among phoneticians that for many speakers long vowels in Icelandic tend to diphthongize. It is not always possible to distinguish between regular diphthongization and the beginning stages of Flámæli.' [author's translation]

Björn Guðfinnsson also collapses 'unclear' Flámæli with regular Flámæli. In our data only one male informant seemed to fall into this category. It was thus deemed unnecessary to account for this informant's speech separately.

The different linguistic contexts that are thought to have affected Flámæli in Icelandic in Iceland are discussed separately below. The review of previous studies of Flámæli is followed by a discussion on how the study of Flámæli in NA Icelandic might add to previous findings.

The Effect of Vowel Quantity

The single most important factor that influences the appearance of Flámæli in the studies in Iceland is vowel length. Length in Icelandic is determined by syllable weight and stress. The general rule of stress assignment in Icelandic is: *primary stress falls on the first syllable in non-compound words and on every second syllable after that*. In compound words primary stress falls on the first syllable of the first word, but heavy secondary stress falls on the first syllable of the second word in the compound (Kristján Árnason 1983).

Examples:

1hamar2inn   the hammer   non-compound
1forða1búr   storage room   compound

Length is determined by syllable weight in that vowels are long in stressed syllables if followed by one or no consonant. Conversely, "vowels are short before two or more consonants" (Kristján Árnason 1980, p. 22).

Examples:

vera [vE:Ra] 'to be' vs verra [vER:a] 'worse'
mun [mY:n] 'will (v)' vs munn[mYn:] 'mouth (acc.)'

The exception to this rule is that vowels are long before two consonant clusters containing (p, t, k, s) + (v, j, r) (Kristján Árnason 1980, p. 22).

Examples:

nepja [nE:pja] 'cold weather'
skrökva [skRö:kva] 'to lie'

The optimal conditions for Flámæli seem to be for long vowels in the first, stressed syllable of a word. This is indicated by the diacritic :).

Contrastive stress could affect Flámæli in cases where normally short vowels became long in syllables that are stressed for emphasis. There is conflicting evidence of this in Icelandic. Kristján Árnason (1980) claims that the phonological manifestation of both (lexical and contrastive) types of stress seem to be similar. For example: *mann*+INUM 'man + def. art. (dative)' with a contrastive stress on the second (normally unstressed) syllable is realized with a long [I:] in the second syllable, followed by [n] instead of a normally short [I] (p. 14). Höskuldur Þráinsson (1985) supports this view. Magnús Pétursson (1978) measured the duration of the vowel in stressed syllables and found that in most cases they did lengthen with contrastive stress (pp. 36–37), although long vowels lengthened more than short vowels. However, Ari Páll Kristinsson et al. (1987), who also measured vowel length in contrastive stress, found that vowels in the syllable type VC: (short V) did not lengthen substantially with contrastive stress, nor did they lengthen in slow speech: Ari Páll Kristinsson et al. (1987) came to the following conclusions:

Sérhljóð sem er hljóðkerfislega stutt (VC:) tekur nánast engum breytingum í áherslu og litlum í hægu tali. (p. 29)

'Vowels that are phonologically short (VC:) undergo hardly any change with (contrastive) stress and very little change in slow speech'. [author's translation]

The data from NA Icelandic seems to support the claims of Kristján Árnason, Höskuldur Þráinsson, and Magnús Pétursson in that there are several instances where normally short vowels are lengthened with contrastive stress, thus creating the conditions for Flámæli to occur (stressed word is underlined):

Example:

Sr. Magnús var á móti þessi eilífri <u>synd</u> [sI:nd]
'Pastor Magnús was against this eternal <u>sin</u>'

Since there is some evidence to support the claim that normally short vowels can lengthen with contrastive stress, this may account for some examples of Flámæli in apparently short vowels in previous studies, as well as in this one, although that would be difficult to substantiate without detailed spectrographic measurements.

Although Björn Guðfinnsson found that Flámæli was generally confined to long vowels, he claimed that Flámæli was also found in the short variants "although not very frequently; yet" (1946, p. 56) [author's translation]. Björn Guðfinnsson seemed to believe that Flámæli would indeed spread to the short variants, given enough time. A study under his direction, but not conducted by himself, on Flámæli in short vowels revealed Flámæli in the written language of forty-two out of the fifty-eight children tested. A subsequent reading test administered to the same children a month later by Björn Guðfinnsson himself revealed "hardly any Flámæli of the short variants" (1946, p. 109) [author's translation]. Björn Guðfinnsson concluded, as modern linguists know, that written tests are not a good indicator of a person's language competence (1946, p. 108).

Some other considerations of the effect of vowel length have been suggested in previous studies of Flámæli (Þórunn Blöndal 1985). One such finding is that Flámæli is more likely to occur in monosyllabic words than disyllabic words.

It is well established that certain environments, certain positions within phrases and sentences, intonation contours, and other factors can affect segmental duration. Liberman (1978) claims that "from a theoretical point of view there is a very serious amount of arbitrariness in any decision about how to interpret duration measurements, even for those cases where measurements are possible" (p. 129).

Autosegmental phonology assumes that short segments occupy one time slot and long segments occupy two time slots, and that these time slots are mediated by the skeletal tier (Clements and Keyser 1983). Maintaining a discrete short-long distinction is especially important in Icelandic as it preserves the weight of the syllable. There are several features of Icelandic that support this type of analysis (see Höskuldur Þráinsson 1978 on preaspiration and compensatory lengthening; Macken 1989 on syllable structure). It would violate the well-formedness principle (Clements and Keyser 1983) if we were to assume that vowel segments could occupy a slot and a half or a slot and a quarter. It would seem that, as far as Icelandic was concerned, a vowel has to be analyzed as either long or short for when a short vowel becomes long, or, vice versa, the whole structure of the syllable has to change as well. Furthermore, the claim that a rule can apply or not apply, depending on slightly fluctuating length difference, seems unlikely. The characteristics of vowel quantity in Iceland support a view wherein vowel length should be kept discrete, either short or long, when they are considered as a factor in the appearance of Flámæli. The alternative would be to consider Flámæli a phonetic process susceptible to co-articulatory effects. Although there is undoubtedly some fluctuation in length of short vowels and long vowels, depending on the linguistic context, the basic length distinctions must be preserved in Icelandic in order to maintain the weight of the syllable.

Vowel length was thus chosen as an important linguistic factor in affecting the probability of Flámæli's occurring. Vowel length was determined by the basic rule for vowel length stated at the beginning of this section. If Flámæli were likely to spread to the short variants, as Björn Guðfinnsson suggested, it would be likely to do so in NA Icelandic, with its narrowing functional range and status as a dying immigrant language.

Effect of the Preceding and Following Segment

Björn Guðfinnsson's untimely death prevented him from analyzing much of the data he had amassed in his extensive dialect study. From his notes, it seems he was concerned with the immediate linguistic environment of the Flámæli variants. He felt that Flámæli might be context sensitive and that the segment following the Flámæli variants could affect the occurrence or non-occurrence of Flámæli (Þórunn Blöndal 1985, p. 52). Þórunn Blöndal conducted a Flámæli study based on this idea. She studied the effect of Björn Guðfinnsson's three groups of sounds—stops (p, t, k, c); fricatives (ð/þ, γ/x, v/f, s); and sonorants (l, m, n, r). Blöndal concludes that in the speech of her forty-nine informants, Flámæli of [I:] and [Y:] and [E:] was most likely to occur in monosyllabic words when followed by a sonorant, then fricative, and, finally, stop (pp. 55–59). The variant [Y:] appears with most frequency (although much less than that of [I:], which was found to be most prevalent in Björn Guðfinnsson's study forty years earlier). The variant [E:], which appears with much lower frequency than either [I:] or [Y:], was least likely to occur when followed by a sonorant in disyllabic words. Þórunn Blöndal found that the variable [ö:], which had the lowest frequency of occurrence in her study, exhibits a different tendency from the other variables. The least constraining factor in the occurrence of [ö:] was when it was followed by a stop. A following stop was the most constraining for the appearance of the other variants (p. 59).

In this study, the environments of following vowel, voiced segment, voiceless segment, and pause were studied specifically. For this initial study, I thought that starting with large categories of natural classes should lead the way for narrowing down the distinctive feature differences of the segments immediately adjacent to the Flámæli variants. Following Horwath (1985), feature distinctions were kept general. I found that too detailed feature distinctions among factors created too few cells for analysis. The effect of the following features on Flámæli were studied: (1) vowel, (2) voiced consonants [v, ð, γ, l, m, n, r] (y was excluded as words like *stigi* [sti:yI] 'ladder', 'last' *legi* [lE:yI] 'liquid,' and *degi* [de:yI] 'day' are usually realized as diphthongs). Finally, (3) voiceless consonant (ph, p, th, t, c, kh, k, f, þ, s, x, n̦, l̦, r̦) and (4) pause were included. The voicing distinction within consonants was motivated by the fact that most of the Icelandic sonorants have voiceless allophones, and it seemed unlikely that they would have the same effect on the appearance of Flámæli as the voiced sonorants. Earlier studies of Flámæli in Iceland suggested that long vowels followed by voiced consonant might prove to be the environment most conducive to the appearance of Flámæli (Þórunn Blöndal 1985, p. 83). Harris (1985) also seems to feel that the voicing distinction was important in influencing apparent vowel mergers in some British dialects of English.

Although the quality of the preceding segment has not been considered as a factor in the appearance of Flámæli, preceding segment was included as a factor in this study; i.e., vowel, consonant, or pause.

FLÁMÆLI IN NORTH AMERICAN ICELANDIC

The main discussion of the relationship between Flámæli in Iceland and Flámæli in NA Icelandic appears below. At this point, it suffices to say that Flámæli was brought to North America in the speech of the first immigrants, and survived and spread due to the narrowing functional range of the dying immigrant language (Birna Arnbjörnsdóttir 1989). Flámæli in NA Icelandic can thus safely be assumed to have the same linguistic and social origin as Flámæli in Icelandic spoken in Iceland. Extensive contact with English may further encourage these phenomena in NA Icelandic, especially for (Y). The English mid, tense vowel (^) is close to the mid, rounded (ö) in Icelandic and may be realized as such by some informants. Weinreich (1953) called this process "sound substitution"; i.e., the reinterpretation of a sound in one language with a close but not identical sound in another language. The English mid, tense (^) may thus be the actual target sound for many of the bilingual speakers (Trudgill 1983). The only instance where there is obvious transfer from English is in proper names, which are usually pronounced in their English versions. Example: Gunnar [k^n:aR] becomes [k^n:ər] and Hulda [hYlda] becomes [h^lda].

Finally, there is an unrelated phonetic development in NA Icelandic, which affects the Flámæli rule indirectly. This is the unrounding of (ö) to (E), which is discussed in Chapter 5.

The Social Context of Flámæli

Icelandic is a conservative language with little dialectal variation. For a long time, the existence of dialects in Icelandic was debated, the contention among most Icelandic linguists being that there were no dialects in Icelandic. Up until the last decade, the existence of social variation in Icelandic was a matter of dispute (Gísli Pálsson 1989). The result is that, even though the linguistic history of Icelandic is well documented, there has been little interest among scholars in the geographical and especially the social variance within Icelandic, nor in the influences of that variance on the evolution of the language. As a result, few studies have been undertaken regarding the geographical distribution and none on the social distribution of Flámæli in Icelandic.

Geographical Spread of Flámæli in Iceland and to North American Icelandic

The earliest known documentation of Flámæli dates back to the middle or early part of the last century. The first indirect mention of the feature comes from Gröndal (1885) and Arpi (1886) (cited in Guðvarður Gunnlaugsson 1986, p. 210), at the height of emigration to North America. Very little is known about the origin and initial spread of Flámæli. Björn Guðfinnsson (1946, 1964) studied the geographical distribution of Flámæli by testing about one in every twelve Icelanders, mostly children between the ages of ten and thirteen (1946, p. 97). He found Flámæli in three different regions of Iceland: in eastern Iceland (Austfirðir) where over 60% of those tested had some form of Flámæli; in the northwest (Hrútafjörður) where 30% demonstrated Flámæli; and in southwestern Iceland where 55% of the subjects had Flámæli. Other areas of Iceland were thought to be virtually free of Flámæli.

In eastern and northwestern Iceland, Flámæli extended only to the lowering of [I:] and [Y:], whereas in the southwest, this feature was extended to the raising of [E:] and [ö:] and was found in the short variants as well, although in very limited numbers. The highest concentrations of Flámæli were found in the villages and towns towards the centres of the Flámæli areas in the southwest and the east. The majority of the over 14,000 emigrants to North America came from areas in the northeastern and eastern parts of Iceland. The emigrants from the eastern fjords brought Flámæli with them to North America. The distribution of the emigrants (as presented by Júníus Kristjánsson 1983) and the distribution of Flámæli in the 1940s is demonstrated in Figure 3. As to how many emigrants actually had Flámæli, one can only infer roughly from looking at where they came from and how widespread Flámæli is likely to have been at that time.

FIGURE 3

The Origins of Icelandic Emigrants Superimposed onto a Flámæli Dialect Map

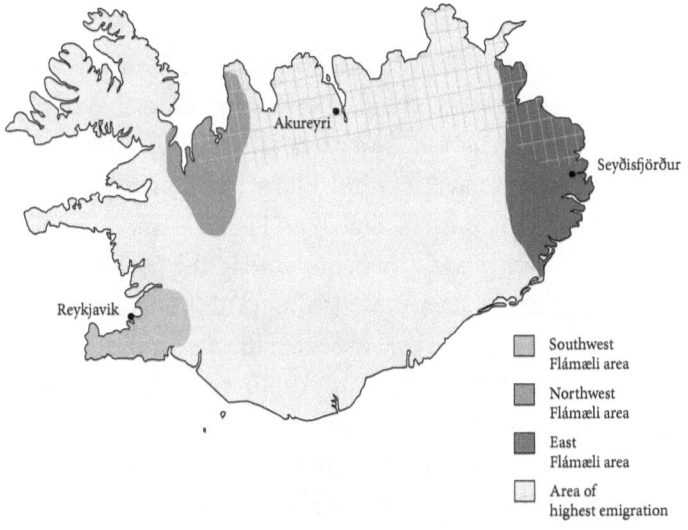

Björn Guðfinnsson's study took place in 1941, or sixty-two years after the first emigrants left Iceland in 1873. In 1941 Flámæli was believed to be spreading rapidly. The area of highest emigration overlaps with the northernmost part of the eastern Flámæli region where about 57% of the teenagers tested were thought to have some form of Flámæli. Emigrants also left from the other two Flámæli areas but not in the numbers they did from the north, an area that did not have Flámæli. It is safe to assume that at least some of the emigrants had Flámæli. The view that the majority of the emigrants did not have Flámæli is argued in Birna Arnbjörnsdóttir (1989).

In *Breytingar*, Guðfinnsson's (1981) handbook for teachers, first published in 1947, he warned that Flámæli was on the offensive and that speakers transferred the "confusion" on to the orthography, causing misunderstandings and breakdown in communication. He suggested ways in which this phenomenon could be eradicated through the educational system (p. 38).

About a decade la ter, Hreinn Benediktsson (1959a) co mmented that Flámæli is "the only feature of pronunciation which is systematically opposed at all le vels of instruction and education with the result that it has b een claimed that it is losing ground in the youngest generation. The outcome, however, is not certain" (p. 95).

Under the auspices of RÍN (Rannsókn í íslensku nútímamáli), a major dialect survey in Iceland was conducted under the leadership of Höskuldur Þráinsson and Kristján Árnason. As a part of that survey, a study of Flámæli among teenagers in Re ykjavík (within Björn Guðfinnsson's southwestern Flámæli region) in 1984 r evealed almost no Flámæli among informants in the twenty-one to seventy age group, but among the twelve to twenty age group there was a slight tendency to raise [ö:] (112, 1 on a scale of 100–200) and [E:] (106, 6). Their conclusions were that the old Flámæli was receding, whereas a new type of Flámæli has emerged in that the mid vowels, especially [ö:], are now more likely to be raised.

In a study of the speech of 200 children in Reykjavík ages four to six years, Flámæli was thought to be almost non-existent (Jón Gíslason, cited in Ari Páll Kristinsson et al. 1987).

Flámæli in Iceland was ul timately reversed through extensive efforts in education, supported by negative public opinion, so that it is now all but extinct.

The Social Distribution of Flámæli

The social context of linguistic change in Icelandic has largely been ignored until very recently. The prevailing view was that no social differences existed in Iceland and thus no sociolinguistic differences. Recent studies have shown that this is indeed no t the case (Ásta Svavarsdóttir et al. 1984; S igríður Sigurjónsdóttir and Joan Maling 2002).

When a linguistic feature becomes a marker for a certain speech group, and having that marker identifies one as a mem ber of that group, and that group has a lo w socio-economic status, there is e very likelihood that the marker, if it is salient, will become stigmatized (Hudson 1980; Chambers and Trudgill 1980; L abov 1966, 1972a, 1972b; T rudgill 1986; B augh 1980; a nd others). This is the case for Flámæli in Iceland. Through a recent reanalysis of Björn Guðfinnsson's data, a c lear correlation was f ound between low economic status and Flámæli (Gísli Pálsson, personal communication). Þórunn Blöndal (1985) reports that of the informants in the youngest group in the RÍNFlámæli study, there seemed to be a correlation between the degree of Flámæli and the occupation of the informant's father. The lower the status of the job, the more likely there was to be Flámæli. Of the forty-nine informants who had Flámæli, 61.23% had fa thers whose occupations had b een categorized in the two lowest status categories, against 38.77% in the middle and upper status categories (p. 71).

The early Flámæli areas all have in common that they had the beginning of urbanization. The eastern fjords, the northwest, and the southwest all had numerous fishing stations with large, seasonal, transient populations of workers drawn by employment opportunities along the seacoast. This, along with a general romantic view in Iceland that farming and rural areas represented purity and goodness, whereas towns and the fishing stations represented corruption, may have contributed to Flámæli's being stigmatized. It is noteworthy that all three geographical areas had some contact with the outside world, with regular and lengthy stays by French and Dutch fishermen in the east and northwest; Reykjavík in the southwest saw the most foreign visitors. However, although many other towns and regions such as Akureyri in the north and Eyrarbakki in the south also had contact with the outside world, their inhabitants did not have Flámæli. Flámæli became highly stigmatized, the only dialect feature to be looked down upon and thought undesirable.

The Social Status of Flámæli in North American Icelandic

Flámæli spread faster in North American Icelandic than it ever did in Icelandic in Iceland (Birna Arnbjörnsdóttir 1989), and is a marked feature in the Icelandic speech of Americans and Canadians of Icelandic descent. Many of the informants in this study were aware that Flámæli was considered undesirable. One of them was a young university-educated woman who joked about having Flámæli and was very aware of the stigma attached to it in Iceland. During and after these conversations, the Flámæli features in her speech increased, as if to say: "I am an Icelandic-Canadian and this is how we speak," reminiscent of Labov's young men on Martha's Vineyard (Labov 1972b).

North American Icelandic is not a full national language, and thus is not susceptible to the usual rules and norms of languages whose functional range encompasses all levels of communication. The way one speaks North American Icelandic has very little effect on one's social advancement. Thus, Flámæli cannot be a marker at the conscious level in the same sense as it was in Iceland, but hovers between being an indicator at the unconscious level for some speakers and a marker for others (Chambers and Trudgill 1980, pp. 84–85). Furthermore, as language loyalty shifted and the descendants of the early Icelandic immigrants spread throughout North America, the dense social network that Milroy and Milroy (1985) identify as the force that kept Icelandic from diverging into different dialects disintegrated. Given that Flámæli does not have the same social constraints in North America as it does in Iceland, it is left open to more rapid change linguistically, socially, geographically, and diachronically.

Flámæli and Gender Differences

Numerous studies indicate that women in Anglo-Saxon cultures are the innovators and more frequent users of prestigious forms of language (note that this is not true in general, especially with non-standard forms, as the inception of language change has often been found to be in the speech of children and teenagers) (Trudgill 1972, 1974). Linguists have indicated that this is not the case among women across cultures (Haeri 1989; Walters 1988). Studies on gender differences in speech are almost non-existent in Iceland.

Þórunn Blöndal (1985) found that women were slightly more likely than men to have Flámæli of [I:] and [Y:], whereas men had more Flámæli of [E:] and [ö:]. A recent study of overuse of dative case in impersonal verbs, widespread, but generally considered 'incorrect' in Icelandic, revealed no gender differences in its use (Ásta Svavarsdóttir et al. 1984). If this is so, then Icelandic women behave differently from women in Anglo-Saxon cultures. It thus became interesting to include sex as a factor in this study, for if North American Icelanders still retain the Icelandic language, it would be interesting to examine whether they also retain the linguistic behaviours that go with it.

THE NATURE OF FLÁMÆLI

Vowel mergers are well-known phenomena in the world's languages. Languages frequently show evidence of vowels having merged, eliminating distinctions where they had existed before. The causality and general mechanisms of the mergers themselves are less clear. Martinet (1952) saw mergers as sound shifts; results of changes within sound systems. Trudgill (1983) has proposed two strategies for the implementation of merger: 1) "transfer," which refers to the gradual shifting of a lexical item from one lexical set to another or what Harris (1985) calls "merger by transfer" (p. 297); and 2) "approximation" (p. 93) or "merger by drift" (Harris 1985, p. 297) whereby two vowels gradually approach each other until they merge completely. More recently, Herold (1989) and DiPaolo et al. (1990) have discussed "merger by recategorization."

Apparent vowel mergers have been identified and discussed by Labov, Yeager, and Steiner (1972), Trudgill (1983), and Harris (1985). This is where vowels may approach each other without actually becoming identical and then splitting again. This process is much less documented and can only be studied in progress, as the reversed mergers leave no evidence in latter stages of the language. The most famous examples of reversed mergers are the vowels in the *meat-mate* classes, which merged in sixteenth-century English and separated 100 years later, and the *line-loin* word classes, which merged in the seventeenth and eighteenth centuries and separated in the nineteenth century in Essex (Labov, Yeager, and Steiner 1972, Appendix A). Trudgill (1983) looked at the apparent merger of the vowels in *beer* and *bare* in

Norwich in their social context. He found that the tendency for merger was constrained by stylistic pressures to keep them apart. These classes, which were thought to have merged and then separated, are seen as never having merged at all, but rather kept up distinctions even though they were not perceived by the human ear. Finally, Labov, Yeager, and Steiner (1972) conclude that true mergers are irreversible (Appendix A, p. 294), so alternative explanations must be found for the instances where "mergers" are thought to have been reversed.

Labov, Yeager, and Steiner (1972, Ch. 6) suggest that the vowels involved in apparent mergers never totally merged, but were merged enough to confuse the speakers. This view is supported by cases where speakers judged two vowels to be the "same" on minimal pair or correlation tests, which proved to be distinct upon spectrographic analysis. They also found that the human ear is sensitive to the first formant position, but it is much less attuned to differences in second or third formant positions. They concluded that speakers make small differences in natural speech production, which maintain the identity of word classes, but that the speakers cannot accurately label these differences on conscious reflection (p. 252). Trudgill (1974) reports an instance where the two vowel sounds in *beer* and *bear* may even have passed each other in phonetic space for some of his teenage informants (p. 98).

Nunberg (1980a, 1980b) discusses apparent vowel mergers in some detail. He discards previous suggestions that spelling and dialect borrowing cause reversals of vowel mergers "even when there is pressure from teachers and peers who regularly make the distinction" (p. 225). Nunberg supports the claims by Labov, Yaeger, and Steiner (1972) that vowel mergers that are reversed are not true mergers, and offers a model whereby he illustrates how a vowel might invade the "perceptual space of another vowel" and be perceived as being similar or the same, yet maintain distinctions of which speakers are not consciously aware. Neighbouring vowels and even whole word classes can remain distinct in production, but the limit of production for each vowel falls within the limit of confusability for the other. The speaker reports that they are the same and cannot identify them consistently (Nunberg 1980a, 1980b).

Many unanswered questions remain about the nature, origins, and spread of Flámæli in Icelandic. Studying NA Icelandic where Flámæli is still prevalent may shed light on some of these issues, as well as add to the discussion on vowel mergers and apparent vowel mergers.

Flámæli has traditionally been considered a case of vowel merger where the vowels involved would eventually collapse. This also reflects the traditional view that language is a system with a life of its own and that all changes are internally driven (Martinet 1952). Within this view, Flámæli is seen as an effort to reduce the number of vowels in the Icelandic vowel repertoire. This reduction of vowels results in a mo re equidistant vowel system, changing from a three back vowel and a five front vowel system to a three back vowel and three front vowel system, which is similar to vowel reductions that have been documented in p revious forms of Icelandic (Hreinn Benediktsson 1959b; Magnús Pétursson 1978).

Höskuldur Þráinsson and Kristján Árnason (1984) s eem to echo this view in their conclusions about Flámæli: "It is tempting to attribute both the lowering of the high vowels and the raising of the mid vowels to the same phenomena, and that they are the result of some 'drift' in the front vowels, and could lead to a merger on the one hand of (I) and (E) and on the other hand of (Y) and (ö)" (p. 125). If the vowel system is restructuring itself, both sets of sounds should eventually merge in all en vironments, both long and short.

In this study, the lowering of [I:] -> [E:] is most f requent and the only change that results in elimination of features; i.e., the tense/lax distinction in the high vowels (i) and (I). This variable had by far the widest distribution, geographically, stylistically, lexically, and otherwise in Icelandic in the 1940s (Björn Guðfinnsson 1946, 1964, 1981). If Flámæli starts with the lowering of [I:], that would eliminate the tense/lax distinction between the two high unrounded vowels [I:] and [i:]. The next most frequent variable is the lowering of [Y:].

The raising of the two mid vowels [E:] and [ö:] is far less frequent in the data from Iceland (Björn Guðfinnsson 1946) a nd was f ound only in t he southwest or one of the three geographical areas in I celand. One w ould expect the short variant to eventually lower as w ell. Studying North

American Icelandic provides an opportunity to investigate Flámæli in ideal conditions for rapid spread. If Flámæli were to spread to the short vowels, one would expect to find evidence of this in North American Icelandic.

The loss of feature distinction between the high vowels does not account for the motivation for the "movement" of the other three vowels. A reasonable explanation might be that [Y:] follows [I:] by analogy. This does not account for the raising of [E:] and [ö:]. It has been noted that these two variables have a much lower frequency overall, and were confined to one dialect area in Iceland. Flámæli of [E:] and [ö:] seems also to have "survived" the eradication efforts, and is still found in the speech of some of the informants in the recent RÍN study on Icelandic dialects. An alternative explanation for the raising of [E:] and [ö:] is in order.

Garnes (1976) found a slight difference in vowel quality between short and long vowels. The most pronounced of these is the slight diphthongal quality of the long mid vowels [E:], [ö:], and [o:]. Garnes claims:

> The long allophones of these phonemes have considerably lower F1 values than the short allophones. The directionality of the diphthongization is toward the quality of the short allophones in all the cases. It appears as the initial portions of the long allophones have risen in height and are diphthongized towards the quality of the short vowel. (p. 11)

The long variants of the mid-low monophthongs [E], [ö], and [o] are falling diphthongs. The first part of the vowel is raised, whereas the second half of the long vowel is very similar to the quality of the short variant, which is lower. Garnes did not find this to be the case for [I] and [Y], which have similar quality, irrespective of length.

The effect of diphthongization cannot be ignored in the investigation of Flámæli, nor of vowel mergers in general, and particularly in the investigation of "apparent" vowel mergers. Studying Flámæli in North American Icelandic provides an opportunity to study the effect of diphthongization on the Flámæli phenomenon in more detail than in previous studies. Björn Guðfinnsson did most of his data collecting without a tape recorder, relying on his ear to identify features. More recent studies have been hampered by the fact that they have studied Flámæli post-facto. Also, advances in data sampling methodology have called into question the representativeness of earlier studies.

Another set of questions in this study centres on the geographical and social context of Flámæli. Although the study of Flámæli in NA Icelandic may not explain the specific nature of its inception and spread in Iceland, it may help explain the more general mechanisms of how and why Flámæli spreads and thus give some indication of how this might have occurred in Icelandic in Iceland.

CHAPTER 7 THE SPREAD OF FLÁMÆLI IN NORTH AMERICAN ICELANDIC

In this chapter the variables [I], [E], [Y] and [ö] will be correlated with the linguistic and social constraints described in the previous chapter.

First, the results of the quantitative analyses are presented. Then the variables in their long variants are singled out and correlated with the other linguistic constraints as well as the social constraints. The four variables are then paired according to the direction of their movement; [I:] and [Y:], which are falling, and [E:] and [ö], which are rising, are correlated separately with the linguistic and social factors. The results of this study are compared to conclusions of studies of Flámæli in Iceland. Finally, the contribution of these findings is discussed in terms of the light they shed on the nature and spread of Flámæli, apparent vowel mergers, and on linguistic change in general.

QUANTIFICATION OF [I], [Y], [E], AND [Ö]

The aim of quantitative analysis is to give order to seemingly disorderly linguistic phenomena; i.e., to determine the probability of certain linguistic and social constraints operating on the application of linguistic rules. We are thus able to predict those situations and those environments in which a linguistic rule is likely to occur. In this study, the movement of four variables in their long and short forms, each with two variants, was studied. The eight variants are:

1) [I] and lowered [*I*]
2) [E] and lowered [*E*]
3) [Y] and raised [*Y*]
4) [ö] and raised [*ö*]

The motivation for treating these two processes as a single phenomenon is that in their social and geographical contexts they seem to be seen as connected by speakers and linguists alike.

The variables (I), (E), (Y), and (ö) were coded for their lowered or raised variants (1 for appearance, 0 for non-appearance); this was the dependent variable. Each variant was coded for all six factor groups:

1) quantity: short or long vowel
2) preceding segment: pause, consonant, or vowel
3) following segment: pause, voiced consonant, voiceless consonant, or vowel
4) locality of informant: Mountain or New Iceland
5) sex of informant
6) age of informant: –50, 50–70, 70+

The study included fifteen factors and considered all environments where the lowering or raising of the variables could have occurred. Percentage tabulation was first completed. This was followed by a stepwise multiple regression analysis using Goldvarb on a Macintosh computer.

The first run indicated a knockout factor of vowel as a following segment. This was to be expected, as there are few words in Icelandic and almost none in the data that contain a two-vowel cluster that is not a diphthong. As the program is unable to tabulate the results if the data contains a knockout factor (in this case, not enough tokens representing a factor to influence the Flámæli process), the data was reanalyzed excluding the knockout factor.

The most constraining factor for the lowering and raising of the Flámæli vowels was a short vowel. It was a significant finding to discover that Flámæli was found in only 3% of the short variants of (I), (Y), (E), and (ö), against 28% in the long variants, indicating that there has been little or no spread of Flámæli to the short variants and that the phenomenon was basically confined to long vowels (see Table 4).

TABLE 4
Comparison of the Appearance of (I), (Y), (E), and (ö) in Short vs. Long Vowels

Variant	%	N	Probability
Short	3	307	0.322
Long	28	1016	0.864

N refers to number of tokens. % refers to percentage of vowels with the feature out of all the possible vowels; e.g., 3% of the short variants had Flámæli.

The key output of a variable rule analysis consists of a list of numbers, one associated with each factor that may affect the variable being studied. The numbers are factor weights, indicating the degree to which the factor favours marker presence rather than deletion. The factor weights show that the higher the number, the higher the probability that the dependent variable will occur.

This result coincides with previous studies of Flámæli. Björn Guðfinnsson (1946, 1964) found that Flámæli was almost entirely confined to long vowels, as did Þórunn Blöndal (1985, p. 80), and Höskuldur Þráinsson and Kristján Árnason (1984). Björn Guðfinnsson was very clear in his predictions that Flámæli would extend to the short variants, given enough time, and would eventually lead to complete merger of the two sets of vowels; i.e., that (I) and (E) would merge, and so would (Y) and (ö) (see also Hreinn Benediktsson 1959a).

In this first run, other linguistic environments—i.e., preceding and following environments—were found to be neutral to the occurrence of Flámæli except when followed or preceded by a pause, which constrains Flámæli (see tables 5 and 6).

TABLE 5
The Effect of Preceding Segment on the Occurrence of Flámæli in Short and Long Vowels

Preceding segment	%	N	Probability
Pause	2	186	0.373
Consonant	11	1310	0.570
Vowel	5	13	0.581

TABLE 6
The Effect of Following Segment on the Occurrence of Flámæli in Short and Long Vowels

Following segment	%	N	Probability
Pause	3	145	0.315
Voiced C	9	1063	0.540
Voiceless C	8	301	0.600

The social constraints did not prove much more revealing but the numbers, percentages, and probabilities are included in Table 7 for illustration and for their implications (see Chapter 6). The step-up/step-down analysis that chooses the most significant correlation deemed all the factors to be insignificant in their effect on the appearance of Flámæli except for vowel length.

TABLE 7
Occurrence of Flámæli (I), (Y), (E), and (ö) as Constrained by Social Factors

Factors	%	N	Probability
Locality:			
Mountain	12	816	0.682
New Iceland	5	693	0.406
Age:			
-50	11	486	0.685
50-70	6	529	0.500
70+	6	494	0.392
Sex:			
Male	6	685	0.467
Female	10	824	0.543

Next, tabulation was performed to determine the effects of the linguistic and social constraints on the appearance of Flámæli in long vowels exclusively.

Quantification of [I:], [Y:], [E:], and [ö:] in Long Vowels

There were 8861 tokens of short vowels in this analysis, of which 3% had the Flámæli variants. There were 3580 tokens of long vowels, and of those about 28% had the Flámæli variants. The next computation was thus performed with the exclusion of all short vowels. Surprisingly, this run did not prove very revealing. The linguistic factors were found to be no more significant than on the first run, represented by the numbers in tables 4, 5, and 6 above. Only the social factors seemed to have a slight effect on the appearance of the Flámæli variants in general in long vowels. Gender was found to be a significant factor but locality and age are just under the significance level (see Table 8).

TABLE 8
Occurrence of Flámæli in Long Vowels Depending on Social Context

Factors	%	N	Probability
Locality:			
Mountain	28	492	0.595
New Iceland	24	552	0.428
Age:			
–50	36	306	0.658
50-70	6	403	0.529
70+	0	335	0.394
Sex:			
Male	23	503	0.467
Female	28	541	0.537

Since Flámæli involves a lowering of vowels on the one hand and the raising of vowels on the other hand, it would seem that the two processes might not be constrained by the same linguistic factors. This result supports the suggestion put forth by Höskuldur Þráinsson and Kristján Árnason (1984), and by Þórunn Blöndal (1985) that the lowering of [I:] and [Y:] may not be driven by the same forces as the raising of [E:] and [ö:]. The lack of significant results of this tabulation may then be caused by the linguistic constraints working on the two different pairs evening each other out. Therefore, a third analysis was run, this time to find the factors that influenced the lowering exclusively or [I:] -> [I̵:] and [Y:] -> [Y̵:].

THE LOWERING OF [I:] *AND* [Y:]

This analysis gave slightly more significant results. The following factor groups were selected by the program as being significant to the appearance of Flámæli. They are presented in their order of significance: locality, age, following environment, and sex.

TABLE 9
The Factors that Constrain the Lowering of [I:] and [Y:]

	%	N	Probability
Locality:			
Mountain	50	395	0.608
New Iceland	36	486	0.435
Age:			
-50	51	246	0.626
50-70	35	284	0.536
70+	42	351	0.389
Following environment:			
Pause	16	39	0.213
Voiced C	44	673	0.535
Voiceless C	48	169	0.575
Sex:			
Male	38	448	0.481
Female	45	433	0.523

It is of interest that in NA Icelandic, Flámæli of [Y:] has overtaken Flámæli of [I:] as the most frequent form of Flámæli with [Y:] occurring 44% of the time against 41% of [I:]. In the Icelandic studies, Flámæli of [I:] was by far the most frequent, although Flámæli of [Y:] seems to be diachronically more robust.

Linguistic Constraints

The only linguistic factor group found to affect Flámæli, other than vowel length, was the very slight effect of following environment (see Table 9) in that following pause was inhibiting to the appearance of Flámæli. Þórunn Blöndal (1985) investigated three groups of sounds following Flámæli for their effect on the lowering of [I:], [Y:], and the raising of [E:] and [ö:] separately (p. 53). These were stops, fricatives, and sonorants. Þórunn Blöndal does not make a distinction between voiced and voiceless fricatives; she does not indicate whether she makes a distinction between voiced and voiceless sonorants. She found that a following stop was the most constraining environment to the appearance of Flámæli of [I:] and [Y:], which appeared in 56.05% of words where the conditions for Flámæli were met. Flá mæli appeared in 75.22% of cases where the vowels were followed by fricatives and in 77.65% of cases when followed by sonorants. The numbers were slightly higher for disyllabic words. The fluctuation is a little over 10% between the highest and lowest percentage, which could indicate that manner of articulation is not highly influential in affecting Flámæli.

The results from both studies suggest that the nature of the following phonological segment other than following pause may not be very effective in inhibiting or encouraging Flámæli.

Social Constraints

As seen in Table 9, the social constraints working on lowering [I:] and [Y:] have interesting implications for further investigation. Flámæli is more likely to occur in Mountain, North Dakota, than in New Iceland. It is more likely to be used by women than men, and there is a gradual increase in frequency from the oldest, through the middle-age group, to the youngest age group, indicating a diachronic spread through the generations.

THE RAISING OF [E] *AND* [Ö]

An examination of the factors that influence the raising of [E:] and [ö:] indicates that there are more instances of the variable [E:] (total 1567) than the variable [ö:] (total 388) in t he data. On the other hand, there were more instances of the raised variant [ö:] than the raised variant [E:]. The results of the tabulations are presented in Table 10.

TABLE 10
The Factors that Influence the Raising of [E:] and [ö:]

	%	N	Probability
Locality:			
Mountain	10	97	0.574
New Iceland	7	66	0.428
Age:			
-50	16	60	0.730
50-70	7	52	0.501
70+	6	51	0.397
Sex:			
Male	6	55	0.417
Female	11	108	0.585
Following environment:			
Pause	9	15	0.465
Voiced C	9	134	0.516
Voiceless C	6	4	0.409

Linguistic Constraints

The nature of the following segment, pause, voiced consonant—or voiceless consonant—seemed to be neutral to inhibiting to the appearance of Flámæli of [E:] and [ö:] (see Table 10). The social context shows similar slightly significant effects as seen for the appearance of [I:] and [Y:] in Table 9.

Notice the much lower instances of Flámæli of the raised vowels seen in Table 10 than the lowered vowels as seen in Table 9. Notice also in Table 10 that a following pause is less inhibiting to the appearance of Flámæli of the raised vowels than voiceless consonant, whereas following pause is very inhibiting to the appearance of Flámæli in the lowered vowels in Table 9.

Social Constraints

The social factor groups chosen as significant for the occurrence of the raising of [E:] and [ö:] were much the same as those chosen for [I:] and [Y:] (see Table 10).

THE LINGUISTIC CONTEXT OF FLÁMÆLI

The conclusions drawn from the study of Flámæli in NA Icelandic diverge in several ways from studies of this phenomenon in I celandic. Previously, Flámæli has been assumed to be an instance of vowel approximations that would eventually lead to vowel merger (Björn Guðfinnsson 1946, 1964; Hreinn Benediktsson 1959a, 1959b; M agnús Pétursson 1978). B jörn Guðfinnsson (1946, 1964) p redicted that Flámæli would spread through linguistic environments, to short vowels ending in merger, and also that it would spread geographically and socially. More recent studies, conducted after Flámæli was r eversed, concentrated on the nature of the Flámæli process. Höskuldur Þráinsson and Kristján Árnason (1984), a nd Þórunn Blöndal (1985) s uggested that the raising of [E:] to [E:] and especially the raising of [ö:] t o [ö:] mig ht be a s eparately driven process. Höskuldur Þráinsson and Kristján Árnason also found that although the "old" Flámæli had more or less disappeared, Flámæli of [E:] and [ö:] was still present in the speech of teenagers in Reykjavík (1984).

Studying Flámæli in NA Icelandic gives us an opportunity to examine the linguistic development of Flámæli unchecked by the language purism policy that reversed its development in Icelandic. Although the spread of Flámæli in NA Icelandic in i ts social context cannot be compared to the possible spread of the feature in I celand, the results from this study can suggest possible directions of the linguistic spread of Flámæli in I celandic in Iceland.

The most important finding of this study is that Flámæli has not spread to the short variants and is still confined to long vowels despite its having spread diachronically, with a grad ual increase in Flá mæli from the oldest speakers to the youngest speakers. This finding suggests that Flámæli is a property of long vowels. Although studies of Flámæli in Iceland have generally been in agreement that Flámæli can also occur in short vowels, albeit in very few instances, only one effort seems to have been made to study this specifically. Björn Guðfinnsson's study in 1945 revealed "hardly any trace of Flámæli" (1946, p. 108) [author's translation]. Of Björn Guðfinnsson's 1588 informants in Reykjavík, only twenty-seven were found to have any degree of Flámæli of the short variants and that included speakers who had as little

141

as one Flámæli feature for just one of the four vowels. In Chapter 6, possible reasons for the apparent appearance of Flámæli in short vowels were presented and will not be repeated here.

Björn Guðfinnsson (1946, p. 38), supported by Hreinn Benediktsson (1959a, 1959b), claimed that Flámæli spread very fast, even to a point that he could see increase in the frequency of Flámæli from summer to summer in certain areas as he revisited the various regions on his study trips (1946). The linguistic and social context of NA Icelandic as a dying minority language constitutes the ideal conditions for increase in the spread of Flámæli (Birna Arnbjörnsdóttir, 1990c). If Flámæli were going to spread to the short variants to allow for complete merger, NA Icelandic seems like an ideal context for this to occur. It did not, which calls for an alternative explanation to the nature of Flámæli.

The second important finding of this study is that the lowering of [I:] and [Y:] and the raising of [E:] and [ö:] show different patterns in that, even though the latter are confined to long vowels almost completely, there seems to be no other significant linguistic factor influencing their development. The frequency of occurrence of raised [E:] and [ö:] is also much lower than for [I:] and [Y:]. This finding coincides with the findings of recent studies of Flámæli in Iceland (Þórunn Blöndal 1985). It is also important that Flámæli of [I:] and [Y:] is no longer found in Icelandic but that Flámæli of [E:] and [ö:] prevails in the speech of some teenagers and that the number of speakers with Flámæli of [E:] and [ö:] seems to remain low but constant, according to Björn Guðfinnsson's findings in the 1940s and through to the results of the RÍN study in the 1980s. Þórunn Blöndal found that most informants who had Flámæli of [I:] also had Flámæli of [Y:] and those who had Flámæli of [E:] also had Flámæli of [ö:]. Björn Guðfinnsson found that Flámæli was limited to [I:] and [Y:] in two of the three geographical areas.

This evidence points to two main conclusions about Flámæli: 1) that the lowering of [I:] and [Y:] is motivated by different factors from the raising of [E:] and [ö:]; and 2) that the raising of [E:] and [ö:] is probably a different linguistic process from the lowering of [I:] and [Y:]. The findings that Flámæli is confined to the long vowels imply that Flámæli is not a case of vowel merger at all but apparent vowel mergers where vowels infringe on each other's phonological perceptual space but never merge. This would explain why it was reversed in a few decades and eradicated with such thoroughness and ease. The following is an hypothesis about the nature of Flámæli based on the findings of this study.

THE NATURE OF FLÁMÆLI

As Hreinn Benediktsson (1959a, 1959b) has suggested, [I:] begins to lower as a result of a "drift" in the language, a continuation of previous vowel changes in the language, which all seem to move towards eliminations of feature distinction. The lowering of [I:] would eliminate the tense/lax feature between the two high vowels [i:] and [I:]. The high frequency of the variant [I:] in the speech of informants in Iceland as well as in North America would support this notion. The lowering of [Y:] does not eliminate a feature distinction as in the case of [I:]. It seems, therefore, that [Y:] might lower by analogy (suggested by Kristján Árnason, personal communication). The lowering of [I] to [E], on the one hand, and the raising of [Y] to [ö], on the other hand, would lead to a more equidistant vowel system. These processes are seen as a continuation of changes that have been occurring in the Icelandic vowel system (Hreinn Benediktsson 1959a, 1959b). It would seem that a pattern exists that lowers long [I:] and by analogy long [Y:] due to a "drift" or diachronic process of restructuring at work in the language. The lowered variants invade the space of their mid counterparts [E:] and [ö:] and they are perceived as the same or similar. This does not explain, however, why [E:] and [ö:] are raised. And the question remains, will this lead to merger?

Long vowels in Icelandic tend to diphthongize. According to Garnes (1976) the long mid vowels [E:], [ö:], and [o:] are sometimes realized as near diphthongs, where the first part of the vowel is raised but the second part has formant qualities very close to the undiphthongized short variants. This means that the long variants of the mid vowels [E:], [ö:], and [o:] are "falling diphthongs with two steady states" (p. 12). Since the first part of the vowel is raised, the [E:] vowel is sometimes perceived as close to an [I:], and the vowel [ö:] as close to an [Y:]. This does not occur with the back vowel [o:], as there are no other vowels near whose "space" could be invaded. There is historical precedence for this type of diphthongization and eventual split of the mid front vowel [E:]. The older long [E:] divided, the first part was raised and became a glide, and the falling second part became an [a] as in *fell-fjall* (Garnes 1976). Notice, however, that [E:] did not merge with [I:]. Garnes's measurements further indicated that the high vowels [i:], [I:], and [Y:] are exempt from this process and do not diphthongize.

The results from this study seem to indicate that Flámæli is indeed a case of apparent vowel mergers. Two main findings of this study support this view. The first one is that Flámæli seems to be confined to the long vowels.

Vowel length is derived in Icelandic from structural specifications on syllable weight; long vowels can only appear in stressed syllables when followed by one or no consonant, with the exception of the combinations (p, t, k,) + (r, v, j) as in *nepja, vökva*, or *sötra*. Previous studies of Flámæli in Iceland (Þórunn Blöndal 1985) had concluded that environments that tended to lengthen the Flámæli vowels were most likely to encourage Flámæli. This study suggests that discrete length distinctions are maintained and that Flámæli is a property of the long vowels. Garnes's (1976) measurements found that a 1:2 short:long ratio is maintained for all Icelandic vowels (p. 13).

The second important finding of this study supports this finding; i.e., that the nature of the following segment does not have significant effects on the appearance of Flámæli.

Diphthongization is a quality of the mid long vowels in Icelandic. The data from this study showed that of the Flámæli variants found in short vowels, only six tokens were of the mid vowel [ö], and thirty-six tokens of the mid vowel [E], or 1% each against 99% of non-occurrence in the short vowels.

Functional consideration may explain why [I:] and [Y:] have not spread to the short variants. The vowels [I] and [Y] are found in the majority of inflectional endings (hence the enormous amounts of tokens in this study). Inflections are word final with unstressed syllables, and thus short vowels. Were Flámæli of [I] and [Y] to spread to the short vowels and eventually merge with [E] and [ö], it would cause immense complications for the morphology of Icelandic; in addition, it would upset the inflectional system in its present form and probably destroy it.

The findings of this study support a hypothesis that Flámæli is a two-part process; the lowering of [I:] and [Y:] as a continuation of changes within the vowel inventory of Icelandic and the diphthongization of the mid vowels [E:] and [ö:]. These two pairs of vowels are perceived as the same or similar in the speech of certain speakers. The lowering of [I:] and [Y:] is prevented from spreading to the short variants due to the enormous functional cost it would have on the morphology of Icelandic.

SOCIAL CONSTRAINTS

The results of the tabulations of the effect of social constraints on the appearance of Flámæli have more interesting implications for further study than actual significant findings. Below is a short discussion of these findings.

Locality

Informants from North Dakota had more Flámæli in their speech than informants from New Iceland. New Iceland is the "heart" of Icelandic culture in North America. New Icelanders are close knit as an ethnic group and for many years they were the only inhabitants of New Iceland, other than a small group of Aboriginal people. New Icelanders have had more contact with Iceland and easier access to "institutions" that promote Icelandic culture in America than their cousins in North Dakota. New Iceland is a "close knit network" (Milroy and Milroy 1987), a close-knit "Icelandic" community that actively promotes its Icelandicness.

In North Dakota, on the other hand, Icelanders were one of many ethnic groups in the region, they were more scattered, and they had less access to Icelandic cultural institutions than across the border in Manitoba. There are no signs around Mountain, North Dakota, that indicate that a specific ethnic group lives there other than a few place names and businesses with Icelandic-sounding names or proprietors.

In Bortoni-Ricardo's terms, New Iceland is more of an "insulated" social network consisting of family, neighbours, and friends, whereas the community in North Dakota is more "integrated," although in this case the setting is rural as opposed to urban, as in the case of Bortoni-Ricardo's informants (Bortoni-Ricardo and Maris 1985). Bortoni-Ricardo showed a correlation between the level of integration of her Caipra speakers and dialect diffusion away from the Caipra dialect norm. The findings of this study support this view as the informants from North Dakota had more Flámæli in their speech than did the informants from New Iceland. This is seen in Table 7, reprinted below:

TABLE 7
Occurrence of Flámæli (I), (Y), (E), and (ö) as Constrained by Social Factors

Factors	%	N	Probability
Locality:			
Mountain	12	816	0.682
New Iceland	5	693	0.406
Age:			
-50	11	486	0.685
50-70	6	529	0.500
70+	6	494	0.392
Sex:			
Male	6	685	0.467
Female	10	824	0.543

Age

There is a slow but steady increase in Flámæli from the oldest to the youngest age group, with the highest jump between the middle group (between fifty and seventy years) and the youngest age group of informants (under fifty). This indicates an increase in the spread of Flámæli diachronically and should come as no sur prise. The younger the speaker, the less firm are his ties t o Icelandic culture and the stronger they are to Canadian or American culture. The younger the speaker, the less likely he is to read and write Icelandic and thus have less opportunity, desire, and need to maintain his I celandic. The younger speaker is also less likely to have as strong ties to the speech community. Often she has gone away to school and is more in contact with people outside the close-knit community of her elders.

Sex

Women of Icelandic descent in North America are more likely than men to use Flámæli. This finding goes counter to most findings on the linguistic behaviour of women in western cultures. It is generally accepted within sociolinguistics and dialectology that Western women are the more likely users of "prestigious" dialect features (Trudgill 1974; Chambers and Trudgill 1980; Hudson 1980). In this study the opposite was the case. Flámæli was a highly stigmatized feature in Icelandic in Iceland and most of the North American informants were aware of this. Clausing (1984) reports the same interpretation of the results of his telephone survey of use and attitudes about Icelandic in the NA Icelandic communities. However, since having Flámæli in one's Icelandic is irrelevant to one's social status in North America, there does not appear to be enough motivation to try to change it.

These findings support notions presented by Ásta Svavarsdóttir et al. (1984), who investigated Icelandic students' use of less prestigious Icelandic forms. They found no gender differences in the language use of their informants. This implies that Icelandic women are no less likely to use less prestigious linguistic forms than men are. From the study discussed here we see that the women of Icelandic descent in North America who have upheld their old language seem to have also upheld the linguistic behaviours that go along with it.

CONCLUSIONS

Studying Flámæli in NA Icelandic allowed us to examine the linguistic development of Flámæli unchecked by the language purism movement that reversed its development in I celandic. This study attempts to evaluate synchronic variation in North American Icelandic and apply those findings to problems of diachronic change in Icelandic. The conclusions drawn from the study of Flámæli in NA Icelandic diverge in s everal ways from other studies of this phenomenon in Icelandic. Some scholars have predicted that Flámæli would spread through linguistic environments to short vowels and also that it would spread geographically and socially. The most important finding of this study is that Flámæli has not spread to the short variants and is still confined to long vowels, despite having spread diachronically; it is used by more speakers of the younger generation than of the older generations. There is no evidence to support a claim that the occurrence of Flámæli is affected by linguistic environment such as the nature of the preceding or following segments. It is well known that certain linguistic contexts may cause slight variation in sound quality and duration. However, this is not seen as having an effect on Flámæli, which is confined to long vowels. Length is derived in Icelandic from syllable weight and the short:long distinction is seen as a suprasegmental property specified by the syllable weight, and thus must be preserved.

The second major finding of this study is that Flámæli seems to involve two separate processes: the gradual lowering of [I:] and [Y:], and the diphthongization of [E:] and [ö:]. Each set of sounds is constrained by different factors. The frequency of occurrence of raised [E:] and [ö:] is much lower than for [I:] and [Y:]. This finding coincides with what more recent studies of Flámæli in Iceland have found: that Flámæli of [E:] and [ö:] prevails in the speech of some teenagers and that the numbers of speakers with Flámæli of [E:] and [ö:] seem to remain low but constant from Björn Guðfinnsson's study in the 1940s and in the RÍN study of the 1980s. Perhaps this is a stable characteristic of informal registers.

The main conclusion is that Flámæli involves apparent vowel mergers where the two high vowels are lowered due to a "drift" in the language towards a simpler and more equidistant vowel system. The raising of the two mid vowels is seen as a tendency to diphthongize whereby the first part of each vowel is raised towards [I:] and [Y:] and the second part falls. The four vowels are seen as invading each other's phonetic space, causing the two sets to be perceived as the same or similar.

This will not lead to mergers. It seems unlikely that Flámæli would spread to the short variants; first of all, because short [E] and [ö] do not diphthongize, and because were [I:] and [Y:] to spread to the short vowels, it would be at a great functional cost. It would severely infringe upon the inflectional morphology of Icelandic because short [I] and [Y] are the two most common vowels in inflections. Finally, positing that there was never a merger involved might explain the ease and quickness with which Flámæli was eradicated with such thoroughness and ease within a few decades.

Apparent vowel mergers are common in the world's languages but they are not well understood. This study suggests that processes such as diphthongization are an important but sometimes overlooked part of apparent vowel mergers.

As a sociolinguistic study, this research is a preliminary effort to investigate social variance in Icelandic. This particular study looked at a specific stigmatized feature prevalent in NA Icelandic. Since the results are statistically weak, they are seen as more suggestive of what forces could be at work in affecting Flámæli.

Flámæli of [I:] and [Y:] in NA Icelandic increases steadily from the oldest to the youngest informants, indicating that it is spreading faster the further the speakers are in generation from the original immigrants. This is seen as a result of shift in language loyalties as the previously dense, isolated social networks that fostered language preservation are disintegrating. Young people leave the community to get an education or to seek employment and modern life demands more outside contact. This is especially true for the immigrant community in North Dakota.

Generally, the informants from North Dakota had more Flámæli in their speech than the informants from New Iceland. Again, the idea of the social network is invoked to explain this difference. The immigrant communities in North Dakota are more isolated from the "hub" of Icelandic culture in Canada, and Icelanders settled among people of other ethnic origins. There is very little outward show of the existence of Icelanders in North Dakota. Quite the opposite is true for New Iceland. This community seems to constitute a dense social network. It is more isolated from the world than Mountain. Icelanders are in the majority and the first ethnic group to settle in the area. It is the heart of Icelandic culture in North America and the Icelandic ethnic origins are advertised. Speakers have close ties to one another. Loose social networks enhance dialect diffusion and thus more Flámæli is found in the speech of the informants from North Dakota.

Finally, the results of this study suggest that NA Icelandic women are more likely to have Flámæli than NA Icelandic men. This speech behaviour goes counter to the behaviour observed in other Western cultures where women are thought to use prestigious forms more than men.

In general, further investigation of NA Icelandic will broaden the research on language attrition, language transfer, and language contact. The description presented in this book is not meant to be exhaustive, but rather is meant to be suggestive of issues that need further study.

As far as Flámæli is concerned, a detailed spectrographic comparison of the Flámæli vowels [E:] and [ö:] and the same diphthongized vowels as produced by a speaker who does not have Flámæli could determine whether the hypothesis presented here has value. A spectrographic analysis that shows the two sets to be the same would support the hypothesis.

The finding that Flámæli of [E:] and [ö:] seems to follow the same although weaker patterns in terms of its sociolinguistic spread as that of [I:] and [Y:] is a weakness in the hypothesis presented about the nature of Flámæli. The explanation offered here is that the two processes seem to be treated as one by speakers and linguists.

The idea of social networks begs further study of Icelandic in Iceland. The Milroys characterized the linguistic situation in mediaeval Iceland as an example of a very dense social network that led to linguistic conservatism. This situation has changed as Icelandic society becomes more complex and government and other institutions supply the support previously provided by the extended family. Centuries of isolation have also been broken, especially after the Second World War. The changing social structure and disintegration of the dense social networks in Iceland should provide a fertile field for further investigation of the network concept and of sociolinguistic variation.

The findings on gender differences in the use of Flámæli support impressionistic studies on the speech of women in Iceland. Flámæli is a stigmatized feature and although it may be less so in NA Icelandic, these findings certainly warrant further study of gender differences in Icelandic. Icelandic women have in many ways a different history from their North American and European counterparts. They came from a rural farming and fishing society into the modern world without the interlude of industrialization or the creation of a bourgeoisie. Women have always been seen as an important force in Iceland from the times of the Sagas up until today. The Women's Party was one of the most powerful political parties in Iceland during the last two decades, forcing the traditional parties to place more women in positions that were likely to lead to parliamentary seats and other political positions. Iceland was never a society where men worked and women stayed at home. The history of women of Icelandic descent in North America parallels the history of their sisters in Iceland. They had voting rights on equal footing with men in New Iceland and they were active in the suffragette movement in Canada. The study of gender differences in speech in the context of the unique history of Icelandic women will add valuable insights into the discussion of gender differences in language.

This study is a preliminary effort at sociolinguistic investigation of a variety of Icelandic, albeit outside of Iceland, using the variable rule paradigm. In a span of fifty years, Icelanders have gone from an isolated rural existence to a modern society with one of the highest living standards in the world. Research on variance in Icelandic should prove a fertile ground for further sociolinguistic investigation.

BIBLIOGRAPHY

Allen, Harold B. 1973. *The Linguistic Atlas of the Upper Midwest.* Vol. 1. Minnesota: University of Minnesota Press.

Árnason, Kristján. 1980. *Quantity in Historical Phonology.* Icelandic and related cases. Cambridge University Press.

_____. 1983. Áhersla og hrynjandi í íslenskum orðum. *Íslenskt mál,* 5. 52-80.

_____. 1986. The segmental and suprasegmental status of preaspiration in modern Icelandic. *Nordic Journal of Linguistics* 9. 1-23.

_____. 1987. Icelandic dialects forty years later: The (non) survival of some Northern and South-eastern features. In P. Lilius and M. Saari (eds.). *The Nordic Languages and Modern Linguistics.* 6. Proceedings of the Sixth International Conference of Nordic and General Linguistics in Helsinki, August 18-22, 1986. Helsinki: Helsinki University Press. 79-92.

Arnbjörnsdóttir, Birna. 1989. Flá mæli í vesturíslensku. *Íslenskt mál,* 9. 23-40.

_____. 1990a. Apparent vowel mergers and diphthongization in North American Icelandic. *New Ways in Analyzing Variation in Language Conference (NWAV)*. University of Pennsylvania.

_____. 1990b. Language variation and language change in North American Icelandic. *Colloquium. Department of English. University of New Hampshire.* Unpublished manuscript.

_____. 1990c. *The Linguistic and Social Context of Apparent Vowel Mergers in North American Icelandic.* Unpublished Dissertation. University of Texas at Austin.

_____. 1991a. The polarization of sound change in different social contexts: the development of Icelandic in Iceland and North America. *Scandinavian-Canadian Studies*, vol. 4. 27-41.

_____. 1991b. Gender and language in North American Icelandic. *Association for the Advancement of Scandinavian Studies in Canada.* University of Kingston, Ontario, Canada.

_____. 1992a. Language contact and language change: the effect of categorical shift in loss of case in North American Icelandic. *Society for the Advancement of Scandinavian Studies Conference.* University of Minnesota. Unpublished manuscript.

_____. 1992b. Linguistic relativity, language contact, and language change. Colloquium. Department of English. St. Anselm College, New Hampshire. Unpublished manuscript.

_____. 1994a. Speaking North American Icelandic. *The Icelandic Canadian.* 11-23.

_____. 1994b. The social context of North American Icelandic. *The Icelandic Canadian.* 185-192.

_____. 1994c. Hún vantaði aldrei að gleyma að tala íslensku: the linguistic and social context of North American Icelandic. Department of Icelandic Language and Literature, University of Manitoba, Canada.

_____. 1997. The life cycle of a language. *Canadian Ethnic Studies*, XXIX, No 3. 31-43.

_____. 2001. Kveðja. *Bréf til Haralds*. Afmælisrit til heiðurs Haraldi Bessasyni sjötugum. Reykjavík: Ormstunga. 38-44.

_____. *Impersonal Verbs in North American Icelandic*. (forthcoming).

Bailey, Charles-James. 1973. *Variation and Linguistic Theory*. Washington DC.: Center for Applied Linguistics.

Baugh, John. 1980. A reexamination of Black English copula. In W. Labov (ed.). *Locating Language in Space and Time*. Orlando, Academic Press. 83-106.

Benediktsson, Hreinn. 1959a. Icelandic dialectology: Methods and results. *Lingua Islandica; Íslensk tunga*, vol. 1. 72-113.

_____. 1959b. The vowel system of Icelandic: A survey of its history. *Word* 15. 282-312.

_____. 1972. The First Grammatical Treatise, University of Iceland. *Publications in Linguistics* 1, Reykjavík.

_____. 1979. A Phantom of a rule: Icelandic vowel shift. *Nordic Journal of Linguistics* 2. 65-89.

_____. 1982. Nordic umlaut and breaking: Thirty years of research (1951-1980). *Nordic Journal of Linguistics*, 5. 1-60.

Bessason, Haraldur. 1967. A few specimens of North American Icelandic. *Scandinavian Studies*, Vol. 39, no. 1. 115-147.

_____. 1984a. Íslenskan er lífs eigari en nokkurt annað Þjóðarbrotsmál í Kanada. Interview in *Morgunnblaðið*, February 12, p p. 64-65. Reykjavík.

_____. 1984b. Að rósta kjötið og klína upp húsið. *Lesbók Morgunnblaðsins*, June 16, pp. 4-5. Reykjavík.

_____. 1984c. Hún fór út með bojfrendinu. *Lesbók Morgunnblaðsins*, June 23, p.11-13. Reykjavík.

Bickerton, Derek. 1971. Inherent variability and variable rules. *Foundations of Language*, 7. 457-92.

Blom, Jan-Petter, and John J. Gumperz. 1986. In J. Gumperz and D. Hymes, (eds.). *Directions in Sociolinguistics: The Ethnography of Communication.* New York: Blackwell. 407-434.

Blöndal, Þórunn. 1985. *Flámæli. Nokkrar athuganir á framburði Reykvíkinga fyrr og nú.* Unpublished BA thesis. University of Iceland.

Bortoni-Ricardo, and Stella Maris. 1985. *The Urbanization of Rural Dialect Speakers: A Sociolinguistic Study in Brazil.* Cambridge: Cambridge University Press.

Brown, Becky. 1989. *Pronominal Equivalence in a Variable Syntax.* Unpublished dissertation. University of Texas at Austin.

Buchheit, Robert. 1988. L anguage shift in t he concentrated Mennonite district of Kansas. *IJSL*, 69. 5-18.

Bynon, Theodora. 1977. *Historical Linguistics.* Cambridge: Cambridge University Press.

Cedergren, Henrietta. 1973. On the nature of variable constraints. In Bailey and Shuy (eds.). *New Ways of Analyzing Variation in English.* Washington, DC. Georgetown University Press.

_____, and David Sankoff. 1974. Variable rules: Performance as a statistical reflection of competence. *Language*, 50, 333-55.

Chambers, J.K., and Peter Trudgill. 1980. *Dialectology.* Cambridge: Cambridge University Press.

Clausing, Stephen. 1984. Dialec t preservation in Amer ican Icelandic: A methodological study. *Word*, vol. 35, no. 1. 76-87.

Clements, G., and S.J. Keyser. 1983. *CV Phonology: A Generative Theory of the Syllable.* Cambridge: MIT Press.

De Boot, Kees, and Michael Clyne. 1989. L anguage reversion revisited. *Studies in Second Language Acquisition.* 167-178.

DiPaolo, Marianna. 1987. Pronunciation and categorization in sound change. In Ferrara et al. (eds.). *Linguistic Change and Contact: Proceedings of NWAV-XVI.* Austin: University of Texas. 84-92.

_____. Alice Faber, and Gerald W. McRoberts. 1990. *Phonation differences and sound change in Utah vowels.* Unpublished manuscript. University of Utah.

Dittmar, Norbert. 1976. *A Critical Theory of Sociolinguistics.* New York: St. Martin's Press.

Dorian, Nancy. 1977. The problem of the semi-speaker in language death. In *Linguistics: An International Review.* 191. The Hague: Mouton.

_____. 1981. *Language Death.* Philadelphia: University of Pennsylvania Press.

Dressler, Wolfgang. 1972. On the phonology of language death. *Papers from the Eighth Regional Meeting. Chicago Linguistic Society.* 448-457.

Eckert, Penelope. 1980. The structure of a long-term phonological process: The back vowel chain shift in Soulatan Cascon. In W. Labov (ed.). *Locating Language in Space and Time.* Orlando, Academic Press. 179-219.

Einarsson, Stefán. 1928. On some points of Icelandic dialect pronunciation. *Acta Philologica Scandinavia,* 3. 264-279.

Eiríksson, Hallfreður Örn. 1974. I nterviews with Canadian Icelanders. Unpublished manuscript. University of Manitoba.

Eyþórsson, Þórhallur. 2000. Dative vs. Nominative: changes in quirky subjects in Icelandic. *Leeds Working Papers in Linguistics,* 8. 27-44. <http://www.leeds.ac.uk/linguistics/research/WP2000/TOC.htm.>

Fasold, Ralph. 1978. L anguage variation and linguistic competence. In Sankoff D. (ed.). *Linguistic Variation: Model and Methods.* New York: Academic Press. 85-95.

_____. 1984. *The Sociolinguistic of Society.* Oxford: Basil Blackwell.

_____. 1985. *Short-cut to IVARB.* Unpublished manuscript.

Ferguson, Charles E. 1959. 'Diglossia'. *Word,* 115. 325-339.

Ferrara, Kathleen, Becky Brown, Keith Walters, and John Baugh (eds.). 1988. Linguistic change and contact: *Proceedings of the Sixteenth Annual Conference on New Ways of Analyzing Variation.* Texas Linguistics Forum, Vol. 30. Austin, TX: Department of Linguistics. UT-Austin.

Fishman, Joshua. 1989. *Language and Ethnicity in Minority Sociolinguistic Perspective*. Gr. Britain: Multilingual Matters Ltd.

Gal, Susan. 1979. *Language Shift*. New York: Academic Press.

Garnes, Sara. 1976. *Quantity in Icelandic: Production and Perception*. Hamburg, Helmut Buske Verlag.

Gerrard, Nelson S. 1985. *Icelandic River Saga*. Manitoba: Saga Publications.

Giles, Howard, and Patricia Johnson. 1987. Ethnolinguistic identity theory: a social psychological approach to language maintenance. *IJSL*, 68. 69-99.

Griffin, Peg, Gregory Guy, and Ivan Sag. 1973. Variable analysis of variable data. In *Language in the Context of Space, Time and Society*. University of Michigan Papers in Linguistics.

Guðfinnsson, Björn. 1946. *Mállýzkur I*. Reykjavík: Ísafoldar- prentsmiðja.

_____. 1964. *Mállýzkur II*. Reykjavík: Heimspekideild Háskóla Íslands og Bókaútgáfa Menningarsjóðs.

_____. 1981. *Breytingar á framburði og stafsetningu*. Smárit Kennaraháskóla Íslands og Iðunnar. Reykjavík: Iðunn.

Guðmundsson, Böðvar. 1995. *Híbýli vindanna*. Reyjavík: Mál og menning.

_____. 1996. *Lífsins tré*. Reykjavík: Mál og menning.

Gumperz, John J. (ed.). 1982. *Language and Social Identity. Studies in Interactional Sociolinguistics*. New York: Cambridge Univerity Press.

Gunnlaugsson, Guðvarður M. 1986. Íslenskar mállýskurannsóknir. Yfirlit og ritaskrá. *Íslenskt mál*, 8. 207-226.

Guy, Gregory. 1987. *Variable Rule Analysis on the Macintosh*. Unpublished manuscript.

_____. 1988. *Advanced Varbrul Analysis*. In Ferrara et al. (eds.). 124-136.

Haeri, Niloofar. 1989. *Diglossia and the Sociolinguistic Variable*. Paper presented at NWAV XVIII, Duke University.

Halldórsson, Halldór. 1979. Icelandic purism and its history. *Word*, Vol. 30, no. 1-2. 76-86.

Harris, J. 1985. *Phonological Variation and Change*. Cambridge: Cambridge University Press.

Haugen, Einar. 1950. The Analysis of linguistic borrowings. *Language,* 26. 210-231.

_____. 1956. *Bilingualism in the Americas.* American Dialect Society 9.

_____. 1971. The Scandinavian languages: Fifty years of linguistic research. In T.A. Sebeok (ed.). *Current Trends in Linguistics* 9. The H ague: Mouton.

Herold, Ruth. 1989. *Using Formant Measurements to Test a Theory of Merger.* Unpublished manuscript. University of Pennsylvania.

Hill, Jane H. 1978. L anguage death, language contact and language evolution. In W.C. McCormack and S.H. Wurm (eds.) *Approaches to Language.* The Hague: Mouton.

_____. 1993. Structure and Practice in Language Shift. In Hyltenstam and Viberg (eds). *Progression and Regression in Language.* New York: Cambridge University Press.

Hjörleifsson, Einar. 1888. Bögumæli. *Lögberg* 1. nr. 39.

Horwath, Barbara. 1985. *Variation in Australian English.* Cambridge: Cambridge University Press.

Hudson, Richard. 1980. *Sociolinguistics.* Cambridge: Cambridge University Press.

Hyltenstam, K., and A. Viberg. 1993. *Progression and Regression in Language.* New York: Cambridge University Press.

Jakobsson, Roman. 1968. *Child Language, Aphasia, and Phonological Universals.* The Hague: Mouton.

Jahr, Ernst Hakon (ed.). 1993. *Language Conflict and Language Planning.* New York: Mouton de Gruyter.

Johnson, J. Sigrid. The Icelandic Collection at The University of Manitoba.

Jónsson, Jóhannes Gísli. 1997-98. Sagnir með aukafallsfrumlagi. *Íslenskt mál,* 19-20. 11-43.

Jordens, P., Kees De Bot, and Henk Trapman. 1989. L inguistic Aspects of Regression in German Case Marking. *Studies in Second Language Acquisition,* Vol. 11, 179-204.

Kartunnen, Frances. 1977. Finnish in America: A case study in monogenerational language change. In B. Blom and M. Sanctes (eds.). *Sociocultural Dimensions of Language Change*. New York: Academic Press.

Kay, Paul. 1978. Variable rules, community grammar and Linguistic change. In D. Sankoff (ed.).

King, Robert. 1969. *Historical Linguistics and Generative Grammar*. Englewood Cliffs: Prentice-Hall.

Kiparsky, Paul. 1984. On the lexical phonology of Icelandic. In C.C. Elert, I. Johansson, and E. Strangert (eds.). *Nordic Prosody III*. Sweden: University of Umea.

Kristinsson, Ari Páll, Friðrik Magnússon, Margrét Pálsdóttir, and Sigrún Þorgeirsdóttir. 1987. Um andstæðuáherslu í íslensku. *Íslenskt mál*, 7. 7-49.

Kristjánsson, Júníus. 1983. *Vesturfaraskrá, 1870-1914; A Record of Emigrants from Iceland to America 1870-1914*. Institute of History, Reykjavík: University of Iceland.

Kristjansson, Wilhelm. 1965. *The Icelandic People in Manitoba: A Manitoba Saga*. Winnipeg: Wallingford Press.

Labov, William. 1966. *The social Stratification of English in New York City*. Washington: Center for Applied Linguistics.

_____. 1969. Contraction, deletion and the inherent variablitity of the English copula. *Language*, vol. 45. 775-762.

_____. 1972a. *Language in the Inner City*. Philadelphia: University of Pennsylvania Press.

_____. 1972b. *Sociolinguistic Patterns*. Philadelphia: University of Pennsylvania Press.

_____. 1980. *Locating Language in Time and Space*. New York: Academic Press.

_____. 1984. Field methods of the project on linguistic change and variation. In J.Baugh and J. Sherzer (eds.). *Language in Use*. New Jersey: Prentice Hall.

_____. 1986. On the mechanism of linguistic change. In J.J. Gumperz and D. Hymes (eds.). *Directions in Sociolinguistics: The Ethnography of Communication*. New York: Basil Blackwell.

_____. 1989. The child as lin guistic historian. *Language Variation and Change*, Vol. 1, no. 1. 85-97.

_____, Malcah Yaeger, and Richard Steiner. 1972. *A Quantitative Study of Sound Change in Progress*. Philadelphia: US Regional Survey.

Lambert, R., and Barbara Freed. 1982. *Loss of Language Skills*. Rowley, MA: Newbury House.

LePage, Robert B., and Andrée Tabouret-Keller. 1985. *Acts of Identity: Creole-Based Approaches to Language and Identity*. Cambridge: Cambridge University Press.

Liberman, Mark. 1978. Modeling of duration patterns in reiterant speech. In D. Sankoff (ed.).

Locke, John. 1983. *Phonological Acquisition and Change*. New York: Academic Press.

Macken, Marlys A. 1989. *Icelandic Coda Rules*. Unpublished paper. University of Texas at Austin.

Maling, Joan. 2002. Það rignir þágufalli á Íslandi. Verbs with Dative objects in Icelandic. *Íslenskt mál*, 24. 31-105

Martinet, André. 1952. F unction, structure, and sound change. *Word*, 8. 1-32.

Matthiasson, John S. 1988. A daptation to an ethnic structure: The urban Icelandic-Canadian of Winnipeg, Manitoba. In E.P. Durrenberger and G. Pálsson (eds.). *Anthropology of Iceland*. Iowa: University of Iowa Press.

Milroy, James, and Leslie Milroy. 1985. Linguistic change, social network and speaker innovation. *Linguistics*, 21. 339-384.

_____. 1987. *Authority in Language: Investigating Language Prescription and Standardization*. New York: Routledge and Kegan Paul Inc.

Milroy, Leslie. 1980. *Language and Social Networks*. Oxford: Basil Blackwell.

_____. 1987. *Observing and Analyzing Natural Language: A Critical Account of Sociolinguistic Method*. Oxford: Basil Blackwell.

Neijmann, Daisy L. 1994. *The Icelandic Voice in Canadian Letters*. Doctoral Thesis. Vrije Universiteit, Amsterdam, Holland.

Nunberg, Geoffrey. 1980a. A falsely reported merger in eighteenth-century English: A study in diachronic variation. In Labov (ed.). 221-250.

_____. 1980b. *Locating Language in Time and Space*. New York: Academic Press.

Oleson, Tryggvi J. 1951. *Saga Íslendinga í Vesturheimi* 4. Reykjavík: Bókafatgáfa Menningarsjóðs.

Óskarsson, Veturliði. 1997-1998. Ske. *Íslenskt mál*, 19-20. 181-207.

Pálsson, Gísli. 1989. Language and Society: The ethnolinguistics of Icelanders. In E.P. Durrenberger and G. Pálsson (eds.).

Pétursson, Magnús. 1976. *Drög að almennri og íslenskri hljóðfræði*. Reykjavík: Iðunn.

_____. 1978. *Drög að hljóðkerfisfræði*. Reykjavík: Iðunn.

Rand, and David Sankoff. 1988. *Goldvarb: A Variable Rule Application for the Macintosh*. Centre de reserches mathématiques: Montréal: Université de Montréal.

Rögnvaldsson, Eiríkur. 1983. Þágufallsýkin og fallakerfi íslensku. *Skíma*, 6, 2. 3-6.

_____. Undated. The Status of Morphological Case in the Icelandic Lexicon. Unpublished manuscript. <www.eirikur@hi.is.>

Romaine, Suzanne. 1981. The status of variable rules in sociolinguistic theory. *Journal of Linguistics*, 17. 93-119

_____. 1984. The status of sociological models and categories in explaining language variation. *Linguistische Berichte*, 90.

Rousseau, Pascale, and David Sankoff. 1978a. Advances in variable rule methodology. In D. Sankoff (ed.). 57-69.

_____. 1978b. The solution to the problem of grouping speakers. In D. Sankoff (ed.). 97-117.

Ruth, Roy H. 1964. *Educational Echoes: A History of Education of the Icelandic-Canadians in Manitoba*. Winnipeg: Columbia Printers.

Salus, Peter H., 1971. Icelandic in Canada; A survey of immigration and language loyalty. In R. Darnell (ed.). *Linguistic Diversity in Canadian Society*. Edmonton: Linguistic Research. 231-243.

Sankoff, David. 1978. *Linguistic Variation: Model and Methods*. New York: Academic Press.

_____, and Suzanne Laberge. 1978. The Linguistic Market and the statistical explanation of variability. In D. Sankoff (ed.). 239-250.

_____, and William Labov. 1979. On the uses of variable rules. *Language in Society*, Vol. 8, no. 2. 189-222.

_____, and Gillian Sankoff. 1973. Sample survey methods and computer assisted analysis in the study of grammatical variation. In R. Darnell (ed.). *Linguistic Diversity in Canadian Society*. Edmonton: Linguistic Research. 7-63.

Sankoff, Gillian. 1980. *The Social Life of a Language*. Philadelphia: University of Pennsylvania Press.

Sapir, Edward. 1921. *Language*. New York: Harcourt, Brace, Jovanovich.

Scotton, Carol Myers. 1988. Differentiating borrowing and codeswitching. In Ferrara et al. (eds.). 318-325.

Shuy, Roger, Walter Wolfram, and Wiliam Riley. 1968. *Field Techniques in an Urban Language Study*. Arlington: Center for Applied Linguistics.

Sigurðsson, Eysteinn. 1986. Athugasemdir um h- og hv-stuðlun. *Íslenskt mál*, 8. 7-30.

Sigurjónsdóttir, Sigríður, and Joan Maling. 2001. Það var hrint mér á leiðinni í skólann: Þolmynd eða ekki þolmynd. *Íslenskt mál*, 23. 123-180.

Sigurðsson, Gísli. 1982. *Viðtöl við Vestur-Íslendinga*. Unpublished interviews. University of Manitoba.

Stefánsson, Vilhjálmur. 1903. En glish loan-nouns used in t he Icelandic colony of North Dakota. *Dialect Notes,* 2. 354-362.

Svavarsdóttir, Ásta, Gísli Pálsson, and Þórólfur Þórlindsson. 1984. F all er fararheill. Um fallnotkun með ópersónulegum sögnum. *Íslenskt mál,* 6. 33-56.

Þór, Jónas. 1980. *A Religious Controversy among Icelandic Immigrants in North America 1874-1880.* Unpublished MA Thesis. University of Manitoba.

Þorsteinsson Þ. Þorsteinn. 1940. *Saga Íslendinga í Vesturheimi* 1. Reykjavík: Bókaútgáfa Menningarsjóðs.

_____. 1943. *Saga Íslendinga Í Vesturheimi* 2. Re ykjavík: Bókaútgáfa Menningarsjóðs.

_____. 1945. *Saga Íslendinga í Vesturheimi* 3. Re ykjavík: Bókaútgáfa Menningarsjóðs.

Þráinsson, Höskuldur. 1976. Dialec tal variation as e vidence for aspiration theory. In Weinstock (ed.). *Nordic Languages and Modern Linguistics.* Austin, Texas: University of Texas Press.

_____. 1978. On the phonology of Icelandic preaspiration. *Nordic Journal of Linguistics,* 1. 3-54.

_____. 1985. Um athugun á framburði og eðlilegt mál . *Andvari,* 27. 110. Reykjavík: Hið íslenska þjóðvinafélag.

_____, and Kristján Árnason. 1984. Um reykvísku. *Íslenskt mál,* 6. 113-134.

_____. 1986. Um skagfirsku. *Íslenskt mál,* 8. 31-62.

Trudgill, Peter. 1972. Sex, covert prestige and linguistic change in the urban British dialect of Norwich. *Language in Society,* Vol. 1, no. 2. 179-195.

_____. 1974. *The Social Differentiation of English in Norwich.* Cambridge: Cambridge University Press.

_____. 1983. *On Dialect.* Oxford: Basil Blackwell.

_____. 1986. *Dialects in Contact.* Oxford: Basil Blackwell.

_____. 1987. *Sociolinguistics*. Gr. Britain: Penguin. <www.umanitoba.ca/faculties/arts/Icelandic/IceCan/language.htm>.

Walters, Keith. 1988. Dialectology. In John Baugh (ed.). *Language: the Socio-Cultural Context*, vol. 4 *of Linguistics: The Cambridge Survey*. Cambridge: Cambridge University Press.

Wang, William S-Y. 1969. Competing changes as a cause of residue. *Language*, 45, no.1. 9-25.

Weinreich, Uriel. 1953. *Languages in Contact*. New York: Linguistic Circle of New York.

_____, William Labov, and Marvin I. Herzog. 1968. Empirical foundations for a theory of language change. In W. Lehman and Y. Malkiel, (eds.). *Directions in Historical Linguistics*. Austin: University of Texas Press. 95-195.

Weltens, Bert, and Andrew D. Cohen. 1989. Language Attrition Research: An Introduction. *SSLA*, Vol. 11, No. 2. 127-133.

Wolfram, Walt. 1973. On what basis variable rules? In C-J. Bailey and R. W. Shuy (eds.). *New Ways of Analyzing Variation in English*. Washington DC: Georgetown University Press.

www.ingramcontent.com/pod-product-compliance
Lightning Source LLC
Chambersburg PA
CBHW032104300426
44116CB00007B/883